GETTING OUT

Expert advice for today's teens!

How one troubled teen took control of his life...
And how you can too!

GETTING OUT
Expert advice for today's teens!

John H. Clark, III

BFG PRESS
HONOLULU

BFG PRESS

Getting Out

Expert advice for today's teens!

How one troubled teen took control of his life...
And how you can too!

Edited by Delia Clark and Destiny Carrillo

Published by BFG Press LLC
Address inquiries to:
BFG Press
P.O. Box 252
Oakton, VA 22124
www.BFGPRESS.com

ISBN 978-0-9820307-1-4

Library of Congress Control Number: 2009900820
Printed in the United States of America

3

AUTHOR PHOTO and COVER ART courtesy of BFG PRESS

Books are available in quantity for promotional or premium use.
Send inquiries to info@bfgpress.com.
10% of all profits are directed to charity.

The SAT® The ACT® are products of The College Board and ACT, Inc., respectively.
Endorsement is neither understood nor implied.

For Brittany

Accept. Adapt. Achieve. [®]

~

John Clark III

Table of Contents

Preface

When Webber showed me the gun, I felt a tinge of excitement that I had never felt before. Just looking at the gun made me feel powerful, excited, and bigger-than-life. Interestingly, that "bigger-than-life" feeling was as accurate as the gun was powerful. For that little ".25 automatic" could easily snuff out the life of anyone who found themselves at the business end of that small, potent pistol. It was shiny, perhaps nickel-plated... with a pearl-white handle.

"Let me hold it!" I exclaimed as I reached for the tiny gun. I say it was tiny because the only guns I had seen before that night were my grandfather's big revolvers, and my father's nine-millimeter semi-automatic. Built more for stealth than power, that little .25-caliber shone brightly as Webber slid the gun from the grungy, white sweat sock and placed it in my hand.

I allowed the rush of power to envelop my marijuana-stoked mind as I marveled at the majestic beauty of the compact killing device. The power was so overwhelming... I felt an urge to simply aim the gun across the parking lot and unload a few rounds into the cars next to us. But I knew I couldn't do that; my mother and father hadn't raised that kind of kid. But, with a gun in my pocket, what kind of kid *was* I?

There I was... sitting in the front seat of my father's 1976 Fleetwood Brougham Cadillac in the parking lot of the Saginaw (Michigan) Civic Center. The year was 1985, and I was living the high life, literally. I was out with three of my friends, and we were celebrating my royal seventeenth birthday. And, as any seventeen-year-old teenager knows, a seventeenth birthday must be celebrated in grandiose fashion. Forget the sweet-sixteen crap; we were hard-core partiers, and this night would not be an exception! In fact, we had enough marijuana and alcohol to support a small college drunk fest; but there were only four of us. Nevertheless, we felt the urge to smoke and drink with reckless abandon.

I thought about tossing one of the empty liquor bottles onto one of the parked cars, but I didn't. I knew I couldn't do that... my mother and father hadn't raised that kind of kid.

But what kind of kid *was* I?

There I was: a former honor-roll, eleventh-grade student, educated on the finer aspects of complementary and supplementary angles, sine waves and story problems involving cotangent, tangent, and the ever-lovin' cosecant. Before my junior year, I was a decent student. In the 8th grade, I was on the football team. And I was quite the track star; I ran the anchor leg on the boys 440 relay... often coming from behind to win the race. I played the lead role in several school plays. And I can honestly say I was part of the "in" crowd – popular but not concerned about my popularity; fun to be around, yet independently fun without a need for others in my company.

Indeed, my mother and father had raised me to be a well-meaning, pleasant, positive-minded kid. Nevertheless, there I was... stoned and bordering on drunk... mesmerized by the small, shiny gun that would soon wreck havoc on my life in a most surprising way. But, according to the simple events recounted above, you tell me... ***what kind of kid was I?***

ACCEPT   ADAPT   ACHIEVE ®

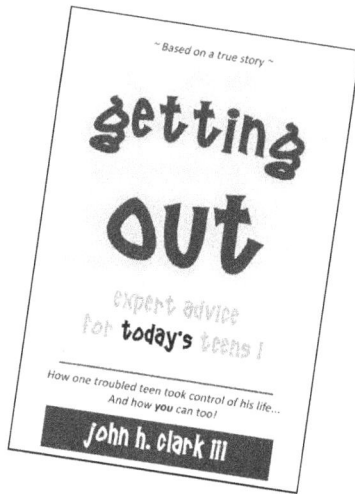

~ Based on a true story ~

getting

out

expert advice
for **today's** teens !

How one troubled teen took control of his life...
And how **you** can too!

john h. clark III

Introduction: Why I Wrote This Book

My Past, My Present, Your Future

I wrote this book for you. You are probably reading this book because of one of the following reasons:

1. Somebody sees something very special in you;
2. You see something very special in the title of this book;
3. Someone recommended this very special book to you.

In each of the reasons listed above, there is a common phrase: very special. Indeed, this is a very special book that is being read by a very special person: *you*. And... this is a very special time in your life. You will never be at this age again. You will never again face the type of change that is about to happen in your life. Very soon, you will face the challenges of adulthood.

Sure, you may already act like an adult. You may even have a few adult responsibilities... perhaps a car, job, or even a child. But having those things is not what determines adulthood. In fact, adulthood means absolutely nothing... unless you, yourself, make adulthood mean something to you. In the preface of this book, I reveal a part of me that was not known by very many people before I published this book.

ACCEPT   ADAPT   ACHIEVE ®

Later in this book, I reveal more about that night and how it changed my life forever. But let's not get ahead of ourselves. For now, just sit back, relax, and know that this book will do for you what I needed to be done for me:

1. This book will tell you the truth about life;

2. This book will explain the world in a way that you can understand;

3. This book will give you a plan... a very *specific* plan to achieve almost anything you want in life.

Let me be clear: I had parents that loved and cared for me deeply. From the time I was five years old, we lived in a nice four-bedroom house in a working-class neighborhood. We lived a few miles from my father's job at a huge General Motors assembly plant.

However, my parents had absolutely no idea how to raise a teenager, much less a teenager with brains and boredom that coursed through my body on a daily basis. You are probably thinking and feeling the same thing: parents just don't get it! They are clueless, clumsy, and clamp down on way too many fun things!

Well, as a guy who's been there and done that, I can tell you this: *you are absolutely correct...* some parents really are clueless! Some really are oblivious to the "real world." And many of them simply don't understand the world in which you live. How can they? They have been transformed into "old people"! They listen to old songs and watch old shows. They say old sayings, but worse yet... they try to use your sayings and end up sounding even more clueless because they say it the wrong way!

How can they be so clueless?

Well, the answer is in the question. Parents are clueless primarily because they don't have the right clues to help them navigate through your young, new, forever-changing world. Adults don't see the constant stream of clues regarding new stuff that you and your friends see everyday.

ACCEPT   ADAPT   ACHIEVE ®

Parents don't hear clues about the latest sayings, and they don't hear the most recently released music – they have their old sayings and favorite melodies to live by. And they are happy with that.

So, yes... you are correct: many parents are clueless when it comes to being a teenager.

But get this: you may be absolutely clueless when it comes to becoming a successful adult. Notice I said "successful" adult. Anyone can be an adult; I have friends that I have known since high school... some of them still smoke massive amounts of marijuana and other illegal drugs. Some still drink and drive. Those same few adults, though much older than you, are not what you or anybody else would call "successful" adults.

So... back to the reason: *Why I Wrote This Book*.

I wrote this book so you can learn from a guy who has been there and done that. I have smoked a few cigarettes, and I have drunk literally hundreds of gallons of alcohol. I have seen friends die, and I have seen friends escape death... if by nothing more than what seemed like mere chance.

And I have seen what can happen when people don't value themselves like they should. On the other hand, I know people who have faced tremendous odds, and went on to live very successful lives. In fact, I am one of those people.

Yes... within these pages, I have literally written the book on how to mess up a perfectly good life... and then make the best of what is left. What's left? A perfectly good life.

I wrote this book for one reason and one reason only...

I wrote this book for *you*.

~ Goals ~

My goal for you is simple:
Finish reading this book

If you can finish reading this book, and if you can follow the simple advice in the final chapters, you will certainly succeed at achieving two very important things:

1. You will achieve the simple goal of finishing this book;

2. You will understand how to prepare for adulthood.

You may be thinking, "_How can he make such a bold statement when he doesn't even know me?_" Well, believe it or not, life is painfully simple. Humans today are not much different than the humans of the 60's, 70's, and 80's. Yes, we now have the Internet. Yes, we now have some truly awesome video games. Heck... we can actually play games over the Internet with people on the other side of the world! So, yes, the world itself has changed quite a bit since I was your age.

But, in general, babies are babies, toddlers are toddlers, teens are teens, and adults are people who forget what it was like to be any of the afore-mentioned types (babies, toddlers, and teens).

So, I may not understand or see the world as you understand and see it... but at least I know and understand the fact that you and I see it differently. I truly respect your view of the world. And I promise not to frown on your view of the world... as long as you don't frown on mine. Deal?

Here's the *real* deal: as long as the ocean is wet, teenagers and parents will struggle to understand each other. This inevitable struggle is simply a natural progression of you...from young teen to older teen; from older teen to young adult; and from young adult to adult. One day, you will be responsible for everything that you do. Believe me: the day will come when you will have the car of your dreams, the house you want, and the husband or wife to complete the pretty picture.

But how does that dream get connected to where you are today?

What do you have to do **today** to get your dream started tomorrow?

Well, for starters, don't wait for tomorrow to start working on a dream that you have today. And, if you don't yet have a dream, let's start there. Let's start with defining your very specific dream. Why is this important? Well, to accomplish any goal, you first have to "set" that goal. And, remember: your first goal is to finish reading this book. So let's write that goal in the space below... go ahead and write your #1 goal on the dotted line:

(*Print your #1 GOAL here*)

(*Sign your name here*)

Did you actually print your goal and sign your name on the previous page? Signing your name may seem silly. However, I am trying to get you to understand a very critical part of the goal-setting and achieving process. The most important part of goal achievement is **stating** the goal. And, to ensure you remember your goals, you should *always* write them down.

~ Always ~

When you actually write down your goals, you transform your thoughts and dreams into reality. Yes, the jotted-down goals are still just a few written words on paper. However, those written words are no longer simply floating around in your head; they are no longer just a dream or a vision.

Those written words are the beginnings of a plan.

*And life really is **just** that simple.*

1: My Story

I was born and raised in Saginaw, Michigan. At the age of five, I was bored with schoolwork. Throughout my formal education, I have always learned things much faster than many of the other kids. I often wanted to talk and play with other kids while they were still doing their own school assignments. The upside, though, was the fact that I had a really smart and caring man for a third-grade teacher... my first experience with a male teacher. And he used multi-colored chalk to draw on the green chalkboards. Wow!

He also taught me how to draw in proper perspective, a skill I proudly use to this very day. I learned quite a bit in his class. And I usually learned at a faster rate than others. I was always fascinated by books about other cultures and countries. I read countless books, including encyclopedias. After a while my parents and teachers realized that I was somewhat of a gifted student. I simply loved to learn.

(Believe me: I am not being a jerk when I say I was gifted. I believe we all have different types of gifts. Some people are gifted with incredible beauty; others are gifted with amazing physical strength and agility; and still others are gifted in ways too numerous to list here. So, when I say I was gifted in my ability to learn, I am not looking down on the learning ability of others; I am merely stating a fact regarding my specific gift. Some people are gifted to play basketball, tennis, or football. Though I played sports, I was far from gifted in anything athletic).

The demographics of my classes in kindergarten through third grade reflected the community surrounding the immediate vicinity of my elementary school – primarily Black and Hispanic, with about a 15% non-minority population mix.

In fourth grade, I was bussed to a predominately white elementary school on the other side of the General Motors assembly plant. My most memorable event at this school was when I practically aced the Michigan State Assessment Test, and was promptly grilled by educators who thought that somehow, this little *Blexican* had cheated on the test.

Interestingly, at the time, I had no idea that mastering a statewide test was such a big deal. After all, isn't that what we were supposed to do? I was also oblivious to the implications the educators were making about me. I was just happy to be in a school that seemed to be a bit more of a challenge than the other school I was at the previous year.

By the time I was in the sixth grade, I was in the "Gifted and Talented" Program, but I was still bored out of my skull when it came to learning new material, applying that new material, being tested on that new material, and then moving on to still more new material. The whole process was simply far too slow for my young, aspiring mind.

The seventh and eighth grades proved to be pivotal. At Ricker Junior High School, I discovered the diverse beauty of girls that had come in from other elementary schools in the school district. I was fascinated by all the different lengths of hair, shades of skin, and shapes of bodies.

There were short girls, tall girls, loud girls, and quiet girls. Some were smart; others were quaint. Some were cute; others were darn right pretty. They *all* fascinated me.

And, to some of those girls, I, the little mixed kid, was equally fascinating. I was handsome. The fair-skinned son of a Mexican mother and African-American father, I had long curly hair when the afro was not yet out of style.

Interestingly, I was not really a Mexican and not exactly an African American. This slight difference from those demographic groups helped me to gain a certain sense of identity that wasn't solely dependent on either race or culture.

I was Black... but not really. I was Mexican, but looked and spoke like more of the Blacks than any of the Mexicans. Thus, I became just "John Clark."

I absolutely loved my status as a "different" kind of young man. My summer tans glowed a beautiful golden brown, and my cousin would often braid my long curly hair.

By the time I reached high school, I had acquired a great deal of attention and notoriety from many people. My older brother and I often took turns driving our father's Cadillac through the park, looking for pretty girls to charm, as we put our new driver's licenses to good use. Girls from other high schools had heard of me. And, to top things off, I now had my own business as a disc jockey. In addition to spinning records at a local club, I was also raking in a couple hundred dollars every other Friday and Saturday night, at party halls, private parties, and basement boogies. I was living the high life... and, yes, I was *way out of control*. But no one could tell me that I was out of control.

For you see, by the time I was a high-school freshman, my parents were in the middle of a family-splitting divorce. Consequently, I, too, was in the middle of the divorce. My parents argued and argued. Sometimes, they were simply too wrapped up in their own lives. Thus, they were not really conscious of my feelings and emotions. And, as I said earlier in this book, parents can be really clueless sometimes.

And, as time went on, my parents were absolutely clueless about my use of illicit drugs and alcohol. I experimented with marijuana. I drank alcohol as a futile escape from the deliberate destruction of my family.

The escape was futile because, though I was entirely capable of doing my class work and homework, the drugs and alcohol soon began to exact a serious toll on my attitude toward school. Attendance took a back seat to alcohol.

Report cards became less important to my parents... So, as you may have guessed, those report cards became even less important to me (the kid who once loved to get all A's).

As a teenage boy, I drank more malt liquor than most people do in a lifetime.

Believe me: I am not the type to exaggerate; and please do not mistake my statements as bragging. Looking back, I am deeply saddened by the memory of such a rapid decline in the value I placed on my life. Initially, I was such a bright, energetic and smart young man. Initially, all I wanted to do was learn about the world and what it had to offer me. Initially, I wanted to do all I could for the world.

But by the time I was a sophomore at Saginaw Buena Vista High School, I was drowning in despair. Despite my profound intelligence, I was not at all concerned about making A's or B's in my classes. In fact, I simply did not care about learning or proving my level of knowledge on a "stupid" test. All I wanted to do was escape the world in which I lived every day. All I wanted to do was live. *I didn't have **any** goals. And I certainly didn't have **any** dreams.*

Much more importantly, I didn't have anyone to guide me in the direction of school, learning, and follow-on educational plans. The guidance counselors at the school didn't seem to offer much help; and why would they? To them, I represented the classic case of an angry kid waiting to explode.

Looking back, I can see that I just needed a mentor. I needed someone to whom I could just say "crazy stuff..." and get away with it. I needed someone who would listen to me and not judge me as stupid, silly, or slow. I needed someone who could offer me guidance without telling me exactly what to do. I needed someone who could laugh *with* me... and not laugh *at* me. I needed a teacher who wasn't being paid to teach me. I needed a counselor who wasn't being paid to counsel me. I needed a school system to understand me... and not a school system that saw me as a problem child. But, back at Buena Vista High School, that's just how they began to see me... as a "problem child." And, sooner than later...

I proved their thoughts to be correct.

~ A Chip on My Shoulder ~

As the bell rang to indicate classes were starting, the students at Buena Vista High School quickly filed into their respective classes, leaving the halls empty and quiet. I had no desire to go to my Algebra II/Trigonometry class, so I simply wandered the halls for a few minutes, looking for someone to "chat up" and pass the time.

In the distance, down the hall, I could see "Martin" headed in my direction. Martin had recently transferred to our high school from a school across town.

As we approached each other, I noted that, if one of us didn't move, we would literally bump into one another. I thought about changing direction. But, I thought to myself, "Then again, this is *my* school. If anything... he should get out of *my* way."

Closer and closer... we walked toward each other.

Our intended paths remained straight as an arrow.

Then... just seconds from walking directly into one another, Martin veered slightly to his right. But the change in direction was just a tad too late, and our shoulders bumped violently, jerking both of us around to face one another.

Furious, I advised him not to do that again, or he would get hurt. He mumbled a few words, and we both went our separate ways. Interestingly enough, a few class periods later, the exact same thing happened. This time, though, I was fully prepared to fight for my personal space and a little bit of respect. I shoved him away from me and snorted, "Let's go – you and me!"

At the time, I was about 5' 10" and 145 pounds. He stood about four inches shorter than I, but was about the same body type. We immediately squared off into a fighting stance, shifting our weight from foot to foot, and waiting for the first blow to be thrown.

I was one ticked off teenager, and I was just about ready to express my level of discontent... when all of a sudden, a mutual friend named Webber stepped in and "broke up" the beginnings of our fight. In fact, I had swung and hit Webber's arm as he jumped in between Martin and me.

22: GETTING OUT

Remember: Martin was about four inches shorter than I; Webber was a few inches shorter than Martin. And there we were, the three of us tangled up in the empty halls of Buena Vista High School, skipping class and creating a lifetime of trouble. But, believe me, the trouble was just beginning.

Martin and I glared at one another. But we again went our separate ways and managed to steer clear of each other until later that night.

Fast forward a few hours to the events in the parking lot of the Saginaw Civic Center...

Soon, we were strolling around in an altered state of consciousness. We were at the Civic Center, high on drugs and missing the first quarter of a great basketball game between perennial rivals Saginaw High School and Saginaw Arthur Hill High School. The Civic Center was packed with just under two thousand teens and young adults, and we were in a foggy haze of stupor.

And I had a "special surprise" in the small, zippered pocket of my parka jacket. Snug and cozy, tucked away in my pocket like a powerful good luck charm waiting for its intended use, that little silver .25-caliber pistol felt good against my chest. And, despite the fact that I had absolutely no plans to use it, I simply "felt cool" walking around all those players, police, and other public people with my little secret tucked away in my jacket.

Though I had arrived at the Civic Center with Webber and two other friends, we each had dispersed, electing to go our separate ways, looking for other, softer, shapelier feminine friends with whom we could spend some quality time. And, as I moved stylishly across the concrete floors of the Civic Center, I felt an increased swagger in my step. I was "packin'," and nobody knew it but me. It was a good feeling. It was also a very dangerous feeling.

And then, as I walked up to the mezzanine level, I saw him... it was Martin, the guy I had bumped shoulders with earlier that day... twice. Wow! This was my lucky day... or so it seemed. I felt a rush of adrenalin as I approached him.

In my mind, the moment was perfect.

There he was, trying to sweet-talk some unsuspecting girl. In fact, he was so wrapped up in conversation with the young girl... he never saw me as I rapidly approached his position.

I rushed up to him and, in a matter of minutes, I had reduced him to a sputtering pile of boy. By crashing into his personal space, I had caught him totally off guard, and I began to verbally whip him with my words. Right there in front of a bright-eyed young lady, I called him all sorts of less-than-honorable names. I pointed my finger within an inch of his nose and forehead as I cursed him loudly and violently shook my hand in his face.

His fear and embarrassment began to feed into my alcohol-induced, egotistically insane sense of self. Martin's fear was obvious, and his eyes searched the area desperately for help.

Sensing that my behavior was drawing quite a bit of attention, I glanced around and decided to abruptly end my little tirade. However, I was not completely done. I looked squarely at the young lady and proudly pronounced: *he's nothing but a punk!* And then I brazenly walked off, proud of my superior performance. And more importantly, convinced that I would not have any more problems with Martin, the new transferee.

As I left the scene, I nodded to a police officer, wondering if he had witnessed any of my overtly aggressive behavior. He nodded back, and I went on to enjoy the second half of the basketball game.

I don't remember which team won the game; I was not really there to see the game. I was more interested in meeting girls and having a good time wandering around the arena. And when the game was over, I started looking around for my three friends. Remember, this was before everybody had a cell phone. At big-attendance events, we found people the old fashioned way: we looked at every single passing face until we found the person we were trying to find.

As I stood in the main lobby area of the arena, I scanned the various faces passing through to the glass exit doors, patiently looking for my three friends. After a few minutes, I thought about simply going back to the parking lot and waiting for my friends at the Caddy. Perhaps they were already there, waiting for me.

24: GETTING OUT

Suddenly, as I turned to search the opposite end of the arena lobby, there I was, face-to-face with Martin again. This time, however, he had two much larger friends standing next to him, and they were all glaring at me.

"Now what's this stuff about me being a punk?" he asked sarcastically. "Not so big now, are you?" he smirked as he gestured toward his two buddies.

"Look, Martin," I said. "If you really want to do something, let's take this outside, right now... you and me. We can settle this one way or the other, just you and me."

At this point, Martin's two friends had stopped three other guys, and they were all glancing at me while whispering to each other. Martin just smiled an evil smile and asked, "What 'cha gonna do?"

I began to repeat what I had said earlier... "If you really want to do something..."

But before I could finish my sentence, one of the other guys in Martin's little gang slammed his fist into my right ear. The powerful blow yanked my head to the left and threw me off balance. Before I could regain my sense of stability, another punch (from one of the other guys) struck me in the jaw... then another fist came in, and another, and another. In a matter of seconds, I went from looking for my friends to getting a serious beat-down.

In a futile attempt at self-defense, I was swinging wildly at anything and anybody that was close to me. I struck a few jawbones and hit a shoulder or two, but I was definitely getting the bad end of this deal. At one point, one of the other guys tripped me, and I fell down amidst a flurry of kicks and punches. Knowing my survival could very well depend on my ability to hit back, I somehow found the strength to get back to my feet and continue swinging.

There we were: a cartoonish ball of five or six teenage boys swarming our limbs toward each other in a sea of hate and discontent. Girls were screaming as a crowd started forming... cheering, jeering, and yelling. For some strange, odd reason, it was the screaming that directed my thoughts from the fight... to the gun in my breast pocket.

For one small split second of time, my thoughts went from "self-defense" to "killer offense."

ACCEPT ADAPT ACHIEVE ®

My hand reached for the zippered pocket just as another punch landed on my head. Instinctively I covered my head with one arm and threw a punch in the general direction of the area where the previous punch had originated.

My fist landed on a nose of somebody. But, believe me: there was no cause for celebration. More and more punches rained on my head and chest. I suddenly realized that I was in a *catch-22*. If I tried to grab the gun, I would open myself up to some serious damage. Moreover, I didn't know anything about the gun in my pocket. Was it loaded? Was it on safety? Was it even really real?

Indeed, looking back, I am amazed at all the different thoughts that went through my head.

The greatest thought, however, proved to be a powerful point regarding that little pistol.

At some point during my teenage upbringing, my father had provided one single solitary piece of advice regarding the use of guns. Quite simply, he said, "If you ever pull a gun on someone, you had better be prepared to use it." And, for some strange, odd reason, my father's words echoed through my mind as I (again) tried to reach for the pocketed gun amid a hail of punches and kicks.

At this point in the fight (if you can call it a fight), my thoughts began to collect and form a sensible plan. As I mentally recalled the words of my father, I also envisioned a likely scenario if, indeed, I yanked the gun out and started shooting.

First of all, if I shot the gun, I would risk killing someone. This was a simple, straightforward fact.

No ifs, ands, or buts about it; if and when you start shooting a gun in a crowded area, you risk killing someone. Moreover, you risk accidentally killing someone who is not related to the fight.

Secondly, when you start shooting a gun in a public place that is well-lit and well-populated by police, you also risk getting yourself killed. Despite what many people think and say about the police, our officers are sworn to protect and serve the public. And, to be sure, if a police officer sees someone firing a gun in a crowd of people, that police officer certainly has a duty to stop that kind of behavior – with or without the use of deadly force.

Interestingly, all these thoughts bounced around in my head as I fought to deal with a gang-style fight while planning some sort of end to the nightmarish ordeal.

Was I really prepared to use the gun? Where was the closest police officer? Did one of the other guys in the fight also have a gun? Did they *all* have guns? If they saw the gun, would they cease and desist with the beat-down, or would they simply pull out their own guns and kill me right then and there?

As the fight spilled across the floor of the lobby area, our cluster of fighting boys soon ran out of room. The collective movement of the fight had moved us over to the glass windows and... *(yes!)*... a glass door; an exit to the sidewalk outside of the arena. Suddenly, I became very aware of what is known as the "fight or flight" response.

The "fight or flight" response is a self-protection mechanism that is preprogrammed into every insect and animal on this planet... including human beings. And, in general, the "fight or flight" reaction is how the body reacts to situations of significant stress. In the most basic definition: whenever you face significant stress, you will either fight... or you will flee. You will either stand your ground and fight; or, if things look horribly bad, you will consider the alternatives and leave... saving yourself for another fight on another day.

As you may imagine, the fight at the Saginaw Civic Center was obviously one of those times when *flight* was a much better choice. Continuing to fight an unwinnable fight was stupid. Fleeing was smart. And I decided to be smart.

As our fighting mob fell toward the glass door, I shoved open the door, fell onto the cold, icy pavement, rolled over several times, and ran. Yes, **I ran**... as fast as I could.

Perhaps admitting to the fact that I ran that night is not the "manly" thing to do. Perhaps I can re-write history in this book and try to make you think I was bigger, bolder, and braver than I was.

Well, I can certainly re-write my version of history.

However, re-writing my version of history will not change the facts of history. And here are the plain and simple facts: I was jumped by several guys, and I was fleeing a mob of angry teenage boys. This is a simple, straightforward fact.

There is no way to sugar-coat that experience. It would be pointless for me to tell you I was not scared. I *was* scared; I was in danger; and I was running for my life.

More importantly, at that point (in my mind), I believed I was also running from the law.

If the police walking around the arena that night had somehow stumbled upon our little fight, they would have arrested all of the participants in the fight, and asked questions later. And we have all seen how the arrest process works: the police tell you to put your hands up, and then they "search" you. Surely, the concealed weapon in my jacket pocket would not have helped my case with the police officers... or the judge that I would subsequently see after being jailed for carrying a concealed weapon.

So, yes... I ran... across the street, down the block, and around the corner. I ran until I was absolutely sure the bad guys *and* the good guys were not following me.

And then I began to get angry.

After finally meeting up with my friends, I gave the gun back to Webber, and then I went home and simmered in my anger. I went home and began to plan for the next day at school. Little did I know that my actions on the following day would change my life forever. What happened next, and what does this have to do with you?

Read on, and you will see.

2: Our Story

My years at Buena Vista High School were some of the best years of my life. Similarly, you are at a very special time in your life. However, you are a teenager; and *all* teenagers go through challenging periods in their lives. I'll say that again: *all teenagers go through challenging periods in their lives.*

Some teenagers have wonderful support mechanisms to help them adjust to these challenging periods. On the other hand, many other teenagers simply don't have access to simple support mechanisms.

What are these support mechanisms, and where can you find them? Well, those support mechanisms come in a variety of solutions, including family members, friends, school counselors, and other community organizations. The later chapters of this book will help you find them.

And if you can't find a good support mechanism where you currently live, visit [www.GettingOut.me], and my associates will help you find the right people and organizations that can assist you in your quest to achieve success.

Missing Mechanisms:
Family

Unfortunately, many of today's teenagers don't have access to these traditionally available support mechanisms. For instance, when I was growing up, I knew my mother and father fairly well. But it seems they did not know me very well. Moreover, though they cared about me and loved me deeply, my parents were far too wrapped up in their feelings toward each other.

And, as is often the case, when parents argue, fight, or divorce each other, the children of those parents often end up being the ones who are affected... in a very negative way. Additionally, because those same parents are so wrapped up in their emotions toward the other parent, many divorcing adults simply fail to see the changes occurring in their children. So, here again, I agree that sometimes parents can be quite clueless.

Other family members can sometimes fill the void of clueless parents. A "cool" aunt or an adult uncle, for example, can sometimes see that your mom or dad is somehow not "there for you." Grandparents, if they are still alive and live in your local area, can also help.

But the fact remains... if your mom or dad is not there for you (physically, emotionally, or mentally), life can present some very serious challenges. And, in some areas of the United States, drug and alcohol abuse by parents of teenagers is quite common. If this sounds familiar to you, please keep reading, your life story begins a new chapter today.

Missing Mechanisms:
Good, better, and best friends

When I was in school, there was a popular Hip Hop song by a group called Whodini. The song was titled "*Friends*," and in the song, the rappers state the following:

> "Friends is a word we use everyday
> Most the time we use it in the wrong way
> Now you can look the word up, again and again
> But the dictionary doesn't know the meaning of friends"

(Friends, Whodini, 1983, Jive/Arista Records
Producer Larry Smith and Thomas Dolby)

The words from that song make a very true statement. Many people say they have friends. Some people say they have "a lot" of friends. But what exactly is a friend? How would you describe your friends? And, as you very well know, there are those simple "friends," and then there are those "best" friends. But, again, what is your definition of a friend?

I only ask this question because friends are people. And people sometimes make mistakes. So, yes, sometimes our friends make mistakes. And sometimes, our friends' mistakes can have a big effect on our own lives. Sometimes, *your* decisions affect other people; and sometimes the decisions of other people affect you.

ACCEPT   ADAPT   ACHIEVE ®

I still talk to some of the friends I had in high school. Actually, some of my current associates are friends I met several years ago while I was in kindergarten.

I still see some of the people I met while in high school. And though I still consider them as friends, many of those friends have a style of living (lifestyle) quite a bit different than mine. Thus, we don't really have anything in common. Some of them have made a choice to continue using illegal drugs. Some of them have made a choice to blame other people for the disappointment in their lives.

Some of them have made a choice to let fear stop them from achieving their dreams. Some of them have made a choice to stop running towards a goal. Some of them have made a choice to remain where they are.

Some of them will never read this book.

But *you* have made a choice to read this book. And you have obviously decided to set a goal; follow a plan to achieve that goal; and... one day... actually *achieve* that goal.

So what's my point? Well, life is actually painfully simple. The events of your yesterday probably affected the events of your today... but not by much. However, your choices, decisions, and actions **today** can have a huge impact on tomorrow, next week, next year... and the rest of your life.

The question is: *how do you want to affect your life?* Do you want to steer it in a positive direction? Or do you want to drive down a dead-end street? Do you want the next five years to end up at a great goal... or do want the next five years to end down a dark hole? Indeed, the differences are clear: goal or no goal; positive or negative; up or down; today or tomorrow... the choice is yours.

Please understand: you may be facing some really, really difficult situations right now. Yesterday, last week, or last month could have been the absolute worst time in your entire life. But all of that can change in a matter of minutes. With a simple plan and a better idea of how to obtain the help you need, your worst yesterday, week, or month will soon be a distant memory that you can look back upon... and actually be proud of yourself for successfully going through it.

And, even if your situation is not yet fully resolved, you can *still* achieve your highest dreams. You can *still* complete your best plans. And you can *still* achieve your biggest goals.

My wife, Delia, was pregnant during her senior year of high school. Sure, she faced a very challenging experience late in her teenage life. And, as an older teenager, she was actually a young adult... just like you.

Today, she has a college degree from Texas A&M University, and she has served as Executive Director of a well-known non-profit organization. Perhaps most importantly, the baby girl that Delia delivered when she was an eighteen-year-old high school student is now a graduate of the University of Michigan.

If Delia had given up on learning and leading a challenged life, she would not have helped her little baby grow up to be a college student.

If Delia had given up on her goals because of the challenges associated with her teenage pregnancy... and the life of being a young single mother, she would not have become Executive Director of a major non-profit organization.

Did Delia face challenges and difficult situations? Of course she did. Did she have to change her plans a few times? Of course she did. Did she face a few disappointments along the way? Of course she did.

But she created an initial plan, and she stuck with it.

She started on a day like "today." She did not wait for the next "tomorrow." And neither should you. Finish this book and start your plan for *Getting Out*. Don't wait to see what your friends are doing. Don't wait for someone to give you something. Don't wait for a magical time to start your plan for *Getting Out*. And, certainly don't wait for tomorrow.

Today is the most important day in the rest of your life.

3: The Big Three

Today matters because all of your tomorrows are affected by your choice and actions of today. Today matters because you *are* a son or a daughter. You *are* a cousin, niece, or nephew. You *are* a friend to somebody, somewhere. Yes... you *are* already a very important person and part of this world. You have a story that is being written as you read the words on this page. And someday you will look back on your most challenging times and say, "Wow, I remember when I didn't have a plan for *Getting Out*."

When you look back, you will see that the world is made up of three very important ingredients. Each of these key ingredients can be considered essential for success. These three ingredients will prove to be overwhelmingly important as we develop your plan for *Getting Out*. These three elements are what I call...

"The Big Three"

1. Education
2. Economics
3. Opportunity

~ The Big Three ~

As I have previously stated in this book, life is painfully simple. Make no mistake; this next chapter is powerfully accurate about the things that make this world go around. There are not many pictures in this book, but all of them are very much related to the content of the book and the point I am trying to make. Take a look at the picture below. The picture below is the *Ideal Equal Opportunity Loop*.

Ideally, *everyone* has equal access to good educational institutions; opportunities for employment (and advanced education); and the economic ability that comes from going to good schools (education) and having a great job (economics). In reality, though, achieving all three parts of *The Ideal Equal Opportunity Loop* can prove to be a difficult task to fulfill, especially if your family has never been strongly suited in any one or more of the three specific areas.

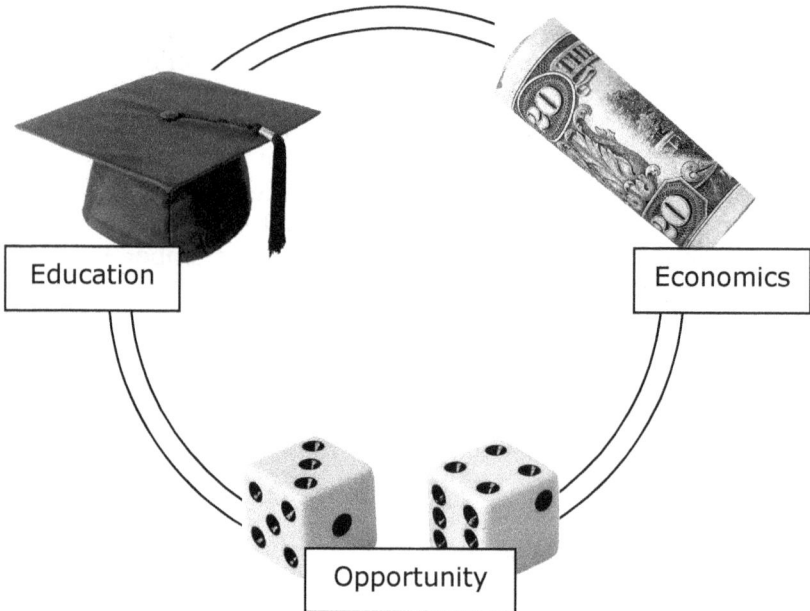

Education

Economics

Opportunity

"The Ideal Equal Opportunity Loop"

© 2009 John H. Clark III

ACCEPT   ADAPT   ACHIEVE ®

Opportunity is represented by the range of options you have available to you throughout your life. The more options you have in life, the better your life will likely be. Like a menu in a good restaurant, the number of possible opportunities you have can have a significant effect on the decisions you make.

If a restaurant has a limited menu, with only a few good meals on it, your opportunity to order, eat, and enjoy different foods is also limited if you eat at that restaurant.

On the other hand, if a restaurant menu has many items from which you can choose, you will enjoy a wide range of opportunities from which you can choose. Think of the opportunities in life like the options available at a cafeteria, compared to the options available at a hot-dog stand. The buffet has many opportunities, and an increased likelihood that you will find something tasty. The hot-dog stand has one thing, with a few variations of the same theme: a hot dog.

Likewise, in your life, do you want opportunities like those available at a smorgasbord buffet? Or do you want the simple lack of alternatives like the meal found in the single-choice hot-dog stand?

This may sound like an oversimplification of life. And perhaps it is somewhat of a dramatic, if not extreme example. However, the main point is this: life is what it is. Either you are working on a plan toward a goal; or you are planning to stay where you are, mentally, physically, socially, intellectually, economically, and, yes... *permanently*.

In this chapter, I am making the simple case that a successful plan in life must consider three very important factors: education, economics, and opportunity. So ask yourself: what is your current situation regarding opportunity?

Do you have the same opportunity as your friends? Do you have the same opportunity as your cousin? Do you have the same opportunity as the girl or boy in the other high schools in your city? **Do you have the same opportunity as the teenager in the other cities of this great nation?**

The short answer is "yes."
The long answer is a bit more complicated.

The long answer reveals that, when considering two specific parts of the "Equal Opportunity Loop" (**education** and **economics**), your specific **opportunity** is often based on those two things. In other words, without a quality education or a good source of income, your opportunities start looking more like a hot-dog stand and less like a smorgasbord buffet.

Ironically, without adequate access to *opportunity*, your access to *money* and *education* also becomes limited. So, in reality, all three of these things (education, economics, and opportunity) are equally important and directly linked to each other. In fact, if you don't have one of the items, the other two items become significantly difficult to get. For example, without a good job, you may never experience the joy of owning your own car, home, or business. Without a good job, the opportunity to travel and see the world is limited. Without a good job, you may not have the ability to support your family and live the American Dream of saving, spending, and someday sending your kids to college. Remember: you will probably be a parent someday.

Like the three separate-but-important wheels on a tricycle... education, economics, and opportunity; all three of them matter. Without a good education, your opportunities in life can become very limited; and your economic situation can become quite a challenge. Can some people do well without a good education? Of course they can! However, education is not just about reading, writing, tests, and grades. In fact, your entire concept of education is about to change as you enter adulthood.

To be sure, riding a bike with three wheels is much, much easier than riding a bike with two wheels. Moreover, riding a bike with one wheel (a unicycle) is harder still! Likewise, if you achieve all three "wheels" of education, economics, and opportunity, life can be *so* much easier! And, yes, riding the bike of life without one or two of those wheels can prove to be a very challenging ride in life!

So the key question is: how can you learn the basics of education, economics, and opportunity?

As a teen, you have been living in relation to someone else's education, opportunity, and economics. As a child, you have been riding the "bike of life" with training wheels. You have spent every year of your life getting your *education* by someone else; being led and fed by the *opportunities* provided by other people; and, yes... you have been taken care of by someone else's *economic* abilities. Remember what I wrote earlier about adults? In earlier chapters, I said, "Adults can be clueless." Well, here's a newsflash for you: **You are about to become an adult!**

Let those words sink in a bit before you read the next few pages. Remember: you have been in school your whole life. During all those years of school, your parents, teachers, principals, and other school administrators told you where to go, when to be there, and when you could leave. You made it safely from elementary school to middle school. And somehow you made it this far in high school. What's next?

Well... here's what's next: *adulthood...* and then you can do almost anything you want! The question is: do you want to be an educated adult with many opportunities and great access to a good job and better money? Or do you want something else? The choice is yours.

Remember: education is not just about reading, writing, tests, and grades. Education can be formal, informal, personal or public. A formal education can best be described as "official." Your high-school education is a type of formal education. As often is the case with formal education, your high school must meet specific requirements and obtain precise certifications in order to be able to give you a diploma.

The G.E.D. Test (General Educational Development) is another formal certification that is available for anyone who has not received a high-school diploma. No matter what...

With help from this book and others...
You can put together a plan and graduate from college.

An informal education is almost as valuable as a formal education. An informal education is gained by paying attention to the things that are going on in your life. In other words, as long as you are learning from your mistakes and listening to the (good) advice of others, you are getting a good informal education.

My grandfather, now dead and gone, was famous for telling long-winded stories that seemed to go on and on forever, without much of a point. But every now and then, he would say something very interesting.

Every now and then, if I was listening instead of mouthing off, he would say something that stuck with me... sorta-kinda' like those famous words that my father said to me regarding what to do if and when you pull out a gun on someone. So, in a very real way, my father and grandfather have given me a life-saving informal education.

Books, newspapers, and magazines also provide a source of informal educational topics. These items, though available publicly, are usually selected as a matter of personal choice. More importantly, you must be very careful when choosing the types of books and magazines you choose for your own informal education.

Remember: as long as you are learning from your mistakes and listening to the (good) advice of others, you are getting a good informal education. Don't make the mistake of learning the wrong stuff from the wrong people.

As you become a young adult, you will begin to interact more and more with full-grown adults. Soon, you will begin to think of high school like you currently think of middle school or junior-high school. Soon, you will begin looking forward to being the magical age of 21. But also keep in mind: You have been in school all of your life. And, like I said earlier, during all of those years of school, your parents, teachers, principals, and other school administrators told you where to go, when to be there, and when you could leave. You made it safely from elementary school to middle school. And somehow you made it this far in high school.

After high school, the whole education process changes. College is not like high school. College is an awesome place.

For those who truly want to learn new things, colleges and universities offer almost unlimited access to everything you ever wanted to know. And for those people who are interested in learning a *little* and partying a **lot**, colleges offer unlimited access to some pretty outrageous parties.

Regardless of what you do in college, though... you *will* learn. Sure, you will continue to learn more about mathematics, literature, and art. But you will also learn about life; you will also learn what you really think about other people and yourself. You will study other cultures, creatures, and comforts of life. If you are from California, you can learn about New York... and perhaps every state in between. If you are from Michigan, you can learn about Malaysia, Mexico, and Morocco. There are courses on chemistry, chemicals, and character. There are classes on creative writing, classical music, and country cultures. There are courses of study on physics, physiology, and physical fitness. Indeed, you can take classes on everything from ants to zebras; art to zoology; and everything in between.

So, yes... in almost any college, you will find a whole new world; a world considerably different than the high-school classes you have recently seen. You will discover a world where there is, undoubtedly, something that will excite you; something that will interest you; and something that will help you rediscover the joy of learning like you did in kindergarten. College is not hard. Like high school, the instructors simply test you on what they have tried to teach you.

The hardest part about college is learning about yourself.

Think about the last few years of your life. Before your high school years, you were in middle school ("junior high" school). And, though you *are* the same person who was in middle school, you have also changed quite a bit since then.

Likewise, by the time you finish college, you will have changed quite a bit again. Perhaps right now you don't think college is right for you. Perhaps you want to join the military or Peace Corps. Great! Make that your goal for *Getting Out.*

My major point is this: you are still changing into a young adult. Don't expect to have life all figured out just yet! Look at the timeline below, and consider how much time you have been in school... basically your whole life! However, at each type of school (elementary, middle school, and high school), you changed from one type of person into another type of person. A few short years ago, you were still a kid!

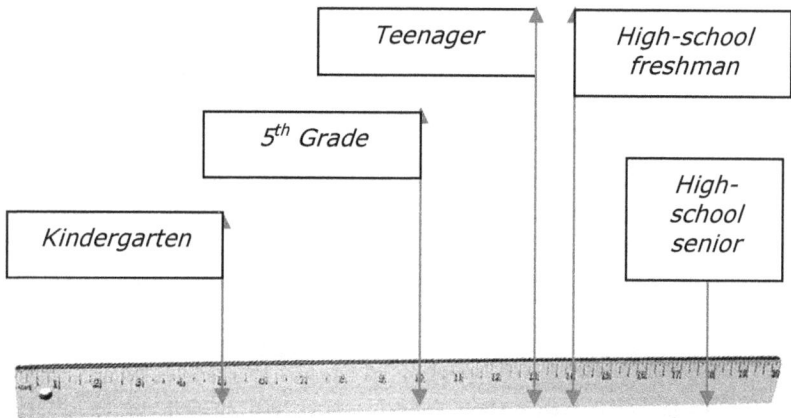

From elementary to middle school, you changed from a little kid into a teenager. From middle school to high school, you changed from a teenager into a young adult.

Next, you are making the transition from young adult... to a full-grown adult. Yes, it *will* happen! And there is absolutely nothing you can do to speed it up or slow it down. In a few years, you will be a full-grown adult. The question is: what are you doing *today* to plan for being a successful adult? *Can you honestly answer such an important question?*

What are **you** doing this week to properly plan and prepare for *Getting Out* of young adulthood and getting into successful adulthood? What are **you** doing to increase your opportunities to become a successful young adult?

What are **you** doing today to focus on the three important parts of the Equal Opportunity Loop? If you are not sure of what will happen next... if you still don't know how this book can help you, read on, and you will see.

Let's Review:

The story of my teenage years includes the following events:

- I had great grades in elementary and middle school;

- My parents went through a family-shattering divorce;

- I experimented with alcohol/marijuana as a teenager;

- My behavior became hostile to others and myself;

So... now that you know some of my story, I am asking you to take some time and think about your own personal story. Perhaps your story reflects a life that is somewhat better than mine. Or, maybe the specifics of your life are far worse than the details I have listed in the previous pages. Of course, there are more details ahead... for both of us.

Looking back, I can clearly see that my brief experience with marijuana had a terrible effect on my judgment and ability to think clearly and rationally. Some people will say, *"How could you admit to such a thing?"* Others may chastise me for putting this information in a book geared towards teenagers. Regardless of what others may say or think about me, this book communicates the truth about what happened to me when I was in high school.

Yes, I made some very bad choices when I was a teenager. Choosing to briefly experiment with marijuana was one of the worst decisions in my life. But I can't change what I did. I can only offer my story as a warning to those who think drugs and alcohol are "no big deal." *Warning...*

Drugs and alcohol can change your life forever.

But a changed life does not have to end there.

In the next few chapters of this book, I will share a few more facts about what happened after my fight at the Saginaw Civic Center. However, understand this: at this point in the book, my life is not complete, and, no matter what has happened in your life... your life is not over or complete.

Indeed, sometimes life can present some fantastically difficult challenges. Sometimes it seems like we should just give up and forget about our plans for the future. Sometimes it seems like no one else in the whole world cares about our problems. Sometimes it seems like our problems are so big... it seems like no one else can understand or help us.

However, no matter how frightening the events of the world appear... sometimes, all we need to do is take a small step back and ask ourselves four simple little questions. Sometimes, all we need to do is *create* a simple plan and then *follow through* on that plan. Today, all you need to do is ask yourself four little questions about your greatest problem. No matter how big you think the problem is; no matter how hopeless the situation appears, simply ask yourself these four little questions:

> *So... what if it **is** true?*
> *What **can** I do about it?*
> *What **will** I do about it?*
> *What **am** I doing about it?*

These four little questions will form the basis for your plan. By asking yourself these four direct questions, you can begin the process of *Getting Out*. What happens next, and what does this have to do with you? Read on, and you will see; when you finish reading this book, you will have a plan for ...

Getting Out.

4: The Bitter Taste of Revenge

After that horrific beat-down I endured at the Saginaw Civic Center, I was hell-bent on revenge. I wanted some get-back, and I wanted it to hurt. I went home after that basketball game, and I sat in our living room seething in anger. My eyes scanned the room as my mind schemed for revenge. I was totally blinded by anger, and I began to care less and less about my grades, my school, and my future.

I guess you could say I began to care more about getting revenge than I cared about getting through life. I was so blinded by anger... I soon found myself focused totally on starting and ending my next fight with Martin. The only thing that mattered to me was getting revenge.

The long-distance future meant absolutely nothing to me.

46: GETTING OUT

The only thing that mattered was the next few hours. I didn't even think beyond the next few days. All I wanted to do was find some way to get back at the guy and his cowardly act. All I wanted to do was prove to the world that I was not a pushover. In reality, nobody really cared about my situation. In reality, the people that saw the fight knew the fight was unfair and lopsided. So, in reality, I didn't have to prove anything to anyone. But there I sat in my living room, convinced that I needed to prove something to the world.

So, the very next morning, I calmly left the house and went to school as if it were any other day of the week. I waited at the bus stop and did not say anything to anyone. In fact, I only did a couple of things differently that day: when I rode the bus, I sat in the very first seat on the bus. I wanted to be the very first person off the bus; I was on a mission.

The January air was bitterly cold that day. And the high-school parking lot was freshly plowed, with small mountains of snow scattered throughout the parking lot. Because of the extreme cold weather, the students were allowed to wait in the school gymnasium until the first-period bell indicated it was time for class.

As our bus approached the front of the school building, I felt a tinge of excitement in my stomach. As I look back on that event, it seems that I somehow knew that the next few minutes were about to have a significant impact on the next five, ten, or twenty years of my life.

I clenched my right hand into a tightly clenched fist. Inside my brown cowhide gloves, I tightened my hand around the brass knuckles concealed within. In case you don't know, "brass knuckles" are a very dangerous and illegal weapon. This is a very dangerous weapon because the wearer of the brass knuckles can literally puncture a skull and not realize the extent of the force and subsequent damage exacted on a person hit by the brass knuckles.

Brass knuckles are formed to fit around a person's knuckles, and, unfortunately, they are specifically designed to focus the force of a punch via a small, narrow contact area... resulting in significantly greater bone, muscle, and tissue damage to the person being hit.

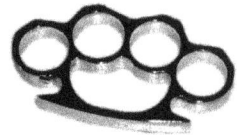

Most "regular" fist fights end with the participants sustaining superficial damage to their respective body parts. Most "regular" fights (those fights not involving weapons) usually leave the participants with little more than superficial skin abrasions or, at worst, bruising of the muscles.

Brass knuckles, on the other hand, can inflict considerably more damage, up to and including the outright fracturing of the bones beneath the cushion of the bruised muscles. Moreover, because of the construction of the brass knuckles, the wearer of the knuckles usually ends up punching harder than usual.

So there I was, brimming with bitter rage. There I was, waiting for that bus door to open, waiting to exact my revenge on my unsuspecting foe.

The bus stopped. The bus door opened. And I quickly bounced down the steps of the bus and onto the icy sidewalk. My eyes scanned left and right, searching for my prey. I was looking for his familiar red jacket. My eyes interrogated every shade of pink, orange, and red... immediately sighting, focusing, and deciding if the person wearing the colors was my intended target.

Martin was not outside, so I proceeded into the school doors and then looked to the left toward the gymnasium doors. Bingo! There he was; Martin was standing just outside the gymnasium doors, talking to Webber.

I launched into a run, raising my fist high into the air. I was on a mission, and nothing was going to stop me.

Just then, Webber spotted my raised fist and pushed Martin towards the gymnasium doors. Just as Webber had shown me the gun during the previous night's activities, I had allowed Webber to see my brass knuckles. We had never used either item; at least not until this moment.

And, because Webber was a mutual friend to both Martin and I, he (Webber) saved Martin from a very serious head injury by pushing him into the gymnasium doors. My punch did, indeed, land on Martin's head, but because Webber had pushed Martin, the punch was more of a glancing blow... and not the devastating punch of destruction I was itching for.

Nevertheless, the push from Webber and the punch from me began a terrific exchange of punches, rolls, and kicks into the gymnasium.

Within a matter of seconds, "ordered chaos" erupted as we spilled into the gymnasium and began a furious fight. Webber tried his best to keep us apart.

But, by this time, almost the entire student body, freshmen through seniors, encircled us, trying to get a front-row view of a furious flurry of punches. (Remember: the students were awaiting the bell to send them to their respective Homerooms).

I honestly thought I was "winning" the fight. Then I felt a shove from the side, knocking me down. And then, out of nowhere, a kick to my chin shredded the inside of my mouth, and burst my bottom lip. Again, here I was fighting more than just one guy. Apparently, another one of Martin's friends decide to toss his fist into the ring. However, this time, there would be no five-to-one fun-run on John's head.

Just as Martin's friend kicked me, several teachers injected themselves into the fight, separating each of us and directing us to our neutral corners. We were pushed, prodded, and dragged to the Assistant Principal's office.

My mouth was bleeding profusely, so I asked if I could stop in the bathroom, rinse my mouth, and get some tissue. My teacher escort allowed me a few seconds to go into the Assistant Principal's bathroom and clean myself a bit. And, in addition to stuffing toilet tissue in between my bottom teeth and bottom lip, I slipped off the brass knuckles and stuffed it in my right shoe.

When I exited the bathroom, I was horrified by the next chain of events.

The principal, in the middle of asking Webber about the fight, noticed a slight bulge in Webber's jacket, and proceeded to pat Webber down.

"What's this, Webber?" he asked.

Everything seemed to move in slow motion as the principal dragged out the grungy sweat sock containing the small silver .25-caliber handgun I had so gleefully handled the night before.

"Is this a gun?" the principal asked in an excited voice.

"Uhm… uhhhhh… It's not mine!" Webber shouted. "I saw it fall on the floor in the middle of the fight!" he said, lying through his teeth.

The principal turned and looked at me. "Is this yours, John?" he asked in a very direct tone.

"Nope!" I said.

"But I tell you what," I said proudly, "…you can go ahead and suspend me right now. I admit it; I started the fight. He had it coming. He and his boys jumped me last night. So go ahead, give me my ten-day suspension and send me home right now."

"Not so fast," the principal said. "First, we need to see whose gun this is."

And so there it was… my future. And there it went… just like that.

In walked the township police, and soon all participants of the fight were transported via police car to the Buena Vista Police Department. In an attempt to discover the owner of the handgun, each of us was fingerprinted and detained while we awaited the outcome of the investigation. I was a nervous wreck as the police read the Miranda Rights to each of us… just in case one of our fingerprints was discovered on the little shiny pistol.

Fortunately, the gun did not have any identifiable prints on it. However, though the gun had been wiped clean of prints, and I was not directly implicated as the owner of the gun, I was eventually suspended from Buena Vista High School for one calendar year. Webber was expelled permanently.

Ultimately, I transferred to another school located on the other side of town. But my story does not end here. Indeed, the physical fighting was over; but a new fight had begun. From the other side of Saginaw, I would soon discover, quite literally, a whole new world.

5: The Other Big Three

Accept. Adapt. Achieve. ®

So... what are *your* current circumstances? What weird situation are you currently in? What unflattering events have occurred in your life recently? What experiences are you dealing with right now, as you read this book? What event is so bad that you "never thought something like this would happen"? As I look back on those days at Buena Vista High School, I remember asking myself a series of questions. Specifically, "How did I end up in a fight like that?"

- How did my grades go from good to bad to worse?

- What happened to my support structure?

- Where were my friends and family?

- Where were my guidance counselors?

- Where was my own sense of self-control?

- How could I be so blinded by rage?

- To whom could I have turned for help?

Like me, you can labor over these questions forever. Like me, you can try to answer these questions. And, like me, you can also "dream up" another 422 questions and try to answer those questions as well. Or... you can simply remember those four little questions:

1. So... what if it *is* true?
2. What *can* I do about it?
3. What *will* I do about it?
4. What *am* I doing about it?

Continuously thinking and wondering about the "why's" is not the answer. Wishing for a change in events is not a great plan either. Like me, you simply cannot change the past. Like me, your future does, indeed, still exist. Your future is still there. Perhaps it has changed a bit. Perhaps your initial plans may start out a little differently.

Or, perhaps you don't yet have a plan, and you simply just need a plan.

Well, regardless of your situation... no matter where you are or what you have done, the first step toward changing your situation is to "accept that the situation is real." The time for pretending and "make believe" is gone. You must start your plan for tomorrow... today.

Why is it so important to start your plan today?

A "*failure to plan*" is the same thing as a *plan to fail*.

And, right now, right here as you read these words, you need to make up your mind to create a plan. Without a plan, you already have a plan: a plan to fail.

But, by taking the time to ask yourself those four little questions ...you have started the beginnings of your plan. So, let's do just that. Let's start by defining what is true. On a clean sheet of paper, write down ten specific things you want to do. Take some time and think about your dreams (they are part of your situation). What kind of work do you think you want to do? Do you want to attend college? What state would you like to live in? What country would you like to live in? What company would you like to work for?

At this point in your life, you can do anything you want. Let me say this again... at this point in your life, you can do anything you want. You may be thinking something totally opposite of what I just said. After all, how can you get to your dreams? Who is going to help you do that? Where are you going to get the information you need to get you to your dreams? What can you do to get started on your path to success?

Well, remember: after high school, the whole process of life changes forever. Indeed, whether you go to college or not, the days of high school are over! And, in a very real sense, "playtime" is over.

So, again, *how* can you get to your dreams? *Who* is going to help you do that? *Where* are you going to get the information you need to get you to your dreams? *What* can **you** do to get *started* on your path to success?

Well, the answer is in the question. You must simply START! And today, you can start by answering those four little questions:

1. So... what if it *is* true?

2. What *can* you do about it?

3. What *will* you do about it?

4. What *are* you doing about it?

What if high-school "playtime" is over? What now? What can you honestly do about planning for your future today?

What will you do next week and next year to increase your opportunities for future success? And the best question of all:

What are you currently doing (right now) to help prepare for a more successful life tomorrow and every day after tomorrow?

~ ACCEPT. ADAPT. ACHIEVE. ® ~

Regardless of where you are in life, and regardless of your situation... the hardest part about life is learning about yourself, learning how to deal with other people, and learning how to accept the reality of your situations. Once you conquer these areas, you can learn to adapt to any situation. And, once you have learned to adapt to various situations, you can achieve anything. Yes: you can achieve anything you desire. As long as you accept and adapt... you will achieve.

This may seem like a super-simple concept. Guess what: it is a super simple concept. However... simplicity does not equal easiness. Just because something is simple... don't assume that it is easy. Using your bare hands and bodily strength to tip over a car, for example, is a very simple thing to do. But is it easy?

Walking from New York City to Los Angeles is a simple concept; but is it easy? Of course not! Here's my point: in the paragraph above, I state, "The hardest part about life is...

1. *Learning about yourself;*
2. *Learning how to deal with other people; and*
3. *Learning to accept the reality of your situations.*

On the surface, those three "learning events" appear quite simple. And, when you really think about it, the first two learning events are things you should have learned in high school, right? After all, in addition to mathematics, literature, art, and science, high school teaches us certain social skills and acceptable social behavior.

So, then, that leaves us with "learning event" number 3: Learning how to accept the reality of your situations. I'll let you in on a little secret: there are full-grown adults who still do not get this one seemingly simple concept. Yes, there are many, many people who refuse to accept the reality of their situation. But here's another newsflash: refusing to accept the reality of your situation does not make the situation "go away." Refusing to accept the reality of your situation does not change the reality of the situation.

On the other hand, once you accept the reality of your situation, *then* you can begin to deal with that situation... whatever it may be! Once you accept the reality of your situation, *then* you can begin adapting to the situation... whatever the situation may be! Once you accept the reality of your situation, then you can adapt to it; and once you adapt to your situation, you can achieve anything you like... whatever you want to achieve!

Here is your plan for life: Accept. Adapt. Achieve.® Think about the last few years of your life. Before you were in high school, you were in middle school (or "junior high" school). And, though you are the same person who was in middle school, you have certainly changed quite a bit since then. Do you remember when you were in elementary school, and you were uncertain about what it would be like in middle school or junior high school? Or, more recently, do you remember when you were in middle or junior high school, and you were uncertain about what it would be like in high school?

At some point, though, all of a sudden, you were in high school, and you began to adapt to the challenges associated with high school. Every teenager has doubts about high school. Likewise, every teenager has doubts about life after high school. But, just like your first year of high school, at some point after high school, you will begin adapting to the challenges of life. You will begin putting together a plan for *Getting Out* of your current situation.

However, first, you must accept a few things about where you are.

Adapt to those conditions that are affecting or keeping you where you are.

And then, you will begin marching in the direction of your achievement. This *will* happen.

Throughout my entire life, I have validated time and time again that the key to life is in one simple action: The act of acceptance. Regardless of the situation, acceptance is the key. Regardless of the people with whom you interact, acceptance is the key. Despite the magnitude of the consequences you may face in your life, acceptance is the key to solving the greatest or least of your problems.

ACCEPT   ADAPT   ACHIEVE ®

Without acceptance, you will continue to live in denial (the opposite of acceptance). Once you have achieved the solo act of acceptance, you can (and will) begin to adapt to those people or events that seem to cause you harm. Once you have accepted and adapted to your given challenges, you will succeed and achieve your heart's content.

Make no mistake: the key to life is acceptance. You simply cannot change what has already happened. And you simply cannot move to the second key (Adapt) until you first accept a few truths about your given situation, regardless of the specific situation.

Think about this:

- The opposite of acceptance is "denial."

- The opposite of adapting is "maintaining."

- The opposite of achieve is "failing."

| ← | Acceptance | | YOU | | Denial | → |

(In which direction are you headed?)

The bottom line:
If you don't plan to accept, adapt, and achieve...
Then you will...

- *Deny* your goals;

- *Maintain* your life where it currently is; and

- *Fail* to achieve your highest dreams.

ACCEPT   ADAPT   ACHIEVE ®

6: The Power of Denial

A classic study in acceptance (and denial) is found in the story of passengers' actions aboard RMS Titanic, a huge luxury ship that sank in the cold waters of the Atlantic Ocean in 1912.

The ship was given the name "unsinkable." Unfortunately, on April 15, 1912, despite being warned that the ship was taking on excessive amounts of water, many of the passengers refused to accept the fact that the ship was sinking. Perhaps you have seen movies or heard the tales of passengers who refused to believe the ship was capable of being brought down by an iceberg. Many of the passengers really believed that the Titanic was actually "unsinkable."

If you were on a ship in the middle of the North Atlantic Ocean (a very cold ocean with big floating icebergs), would you simply wave good-bye and blow a kiss into the chilly night air as your loved one departed on a lifeboat? Would you hold fast to your faith in an unsinkable ship?

Or would you slowly begin to accept reality?

Since the passengers of the Titanic did not accept the reality of the situation, many of the ship's passengers did not adapt to the evolving situation. They did not **accept** the probability that the ship was sinking. And since they did not **adapt** to the life-threatening conditions, many passengers failed to **achieve** a successful escape. They died of denial.

The same can be said for anyone who sits in a smoky room, refusing to accept the likelihood or probability that "where there's smoke, there's usually fire." Accepting the prospect of a nearby fire, one can (and should) adapt to the situation and seek an immediate exit. Adapting to the situation provides a much higher probability of achieving survivability.

There are those who will say that understanding is more important than acceptance. To them I ask, "Do you understand how your television remote works? Do you understand the electronic interaction between the infrared circuitry on the remote and the receiver on the television? Or, like most people, do you simply 'accept' that, if you push the 'on' button, the television will turn on?" Of course, we all accept the function of the remote, regardless of our lack of understanding of its circuitry.

Titanic, smoke, and television... three very diverse topics; each interwoven with the simple concept of acceptance. If you're on a ship in the middle of the ocean, you should probably accept the possibility of sinking. If you are in a smoke-filled building, you should at least consider accepting the possibility of a nearby fire.

You simply cannot change what has already happened. However... *accepting* and subsequently *adapting* to the situation provides a much higher probability of *achieving* success. In other words...

*If **your** life is on fire... or if **your** life is hot enough to keep you in hot water...it's up to*

YOU

to put out the fire!

~ Denial ~

In daily living, specific rules apply. Accept, adapt, achieve.

> *If your boyfriend is "causing" you serious problems:*
>
> *1. Accept the reality of the situation.*
> *2. Adapt; make changes to which you can commit.*
> *3. Achieve resolution to your problem.*

Likewise, if you find yourself facing some rather challenging situations, do not turn or run from the circumstances.

1. **Accept** the reality of the challenging situation.

2. **Adapt**... change your actions and input to the situation.

3. **Achieve** resolution to your challenging situation.

Please note that "accepting the reality" of your situation is not the same as "accepting the situation." If someone is disrespectful to you or harming you in any way, do not tolerate or accept those types of actions. You must, however, accept the given reality... and then you can adapt to the situation.

If your girlfriend, parents, friends, or enemies are causing huge problems in your life... accept the reality of it, and adapt to it by making a plan to move on with your own life. Create your plan to move your life beyond where it currently is. Wishing will not change things. Hope is great; but action is better. And, before you spring into action, you simply must accept the reality of your situation. More precisely, accept the seriousness of your problems; embrace the challenges you currently face. To do otherwise is a self-destructive form of denial. And you should never underestimate the power of denial.

Looking back on the fight at the Saginaw Civic Center, as well as the fight at Buena Vista High School, you can see that I did not achieve the best possible results. In life, there is always a consequence associated with your actions. Sometimes, your actions will result in positive consequences. The positive consequences can be considered achievements. However, when your actions result in negative consequences, those consequences are usually considered penalties or punishments.

While at BVHS, I acted in a profoundly bad way. Ultimately, my bad actions and bad attitude caused a negative application of the (Accept, Adapt, and Achieve) concept:

1. I *accepted* a violent response to my situation.

2. I *adapted* by starting a second fight at school.

3. I *"achieved"* a very negative result of my actions.

Because of the fight I started at school that fateful morning, I was suspended for a whole year. As you can imagine, all of my friends were at Buena Vista High School. All of my favorite teachers were at BVHS. My house was in the Buena Vista School District; and there was only one high school in the district. Quite simply, that one little fight had begun to affect my entire life.

Although the word "achieve" is best used in a positive sense, you can see that my acceptance and adapting of violence as a way to resolve my problems led directly to the "achievement" of negative consequences.

Sure... the fight at the Saginaw Civic Center was started by Martin. The fight was an unfair battle, and I got my butt kicked. But was my thirst for revenge really worth changing schools, friends, and neighborhoods... just to say that I "got some get-back"?

Some people may say, "You should always get your respect." Other people may say, "You can't let others push you around." But, in reality, life is much more important than simple respect or revenge.

After my vengeful fight in high school, I was suspended for one calendar year. I faced an incredibly bad time in my life. And, as I previously stated, my whole world revolved around my life at school. All of my friends were at Saginaw Buena Vista High School. In fact, I had known some of the BVHS students since kindergarten!

Ultimately, I accepted the reality of my situation and subsequently enrolled in a high school on the other side of town. Interestingly, I transferred from a high school with a predominately Black population of students... to a high school with a predominately White population of students. Talk about culture shock!

Now, when I say "culture shock," I am not merely referring to the stark differences in pop music and R&B... or the significant variances in manners of speech and dress... I am also talking about the significant differences that existed within and among the brick-and-mortar buildings of the school buildings in both districts.

Saginaw Buena Vista High School was a decent high school. And I gained some fundamental knowledge at that school. However, I never understood what a "tax base" was until I went to school on the other side of the city. Over on the other side of the river, they had a swimming pool and, accordingly, a swimming team at the school. BVHS did not have a pool; BVHS certainly did not have a swimming team.

The "other school" had wall-to-wall carpet throughout the school. The "other school" had students who went to Cancun and the Bahamas for Christmas break. The "other school" had a student-managed store with candy, snacks, and school supplies (a store where the students learned to handle store inventory, cash sales, and other *managerial* aspects of running a business).

The "other school" was located
a few miles from a golf course and a country club.

The "other school" had the financial backing of a tax base that allowed the "other school" to spend quite a bit more money per student than BVHS was spending on its students. And, yes, "the other school" probably prepared its students for the "real world" a little bit better than BVHS.

Now you can disagree with the facts that I have presented here. And, yes, you can try to minimize my point by saying "none of those points of fact matter." However, here's the reality of any situation: *life is not fair*. Schools everywhere are different. Some are better; some are worse.

And, like I wrote earlier in this chapter:

Accepting and subsequently Adapting to the situation provides a much higher probability of Achieving success.

So... if life is unfair (and it *is* unfair), when are you going to accept that truth? Once you begin to accept the truth that life is, indeed, unfair, you can begin to do something about it. You can begin to adapt to the reality of the situation. And then you can achieve whatever it is that you want to achieve.

What do **you** want to achieve?

The question is... How can we get to the critical point of acceptance, especially when life, at times, seems so unfair, unreasonable, and just plain ol' difficult to deal with? The answer: Accept, Adapt, Achieve. This may seem like I am answering the question with a part of the question. However, it is absolutely critical that you understand the significance of the single, solitary point of acceptance.

ACCEPT
Accept the fact that you are at a very, very special and critical time in the only life you will ever have. After high school, there are no more Homerooms. There is no more recess. There are no more tardy slips and parental excuses. After high school, you set the pace. You ring the bell. You make the plan. You absolutely must accept this responsibility.

ADAPT

Pay attention to the very specific role you play in your life; your own starring role. You are responsible for *everything* you do. You own everything that has happened to you. You own every single thought. You have absolute power to change all your thoughts. Once you have accepted this key concept of life, you are ready to build on your acceptance.

Adapt to the ideas in this book. If you can accept the ideas above; if you can truly accept responsibility for increasing the good in your life; and if you can avoid blaming people for anything that happens in your life... you are already on your way to success. However, you must adapt now; the time to change is now. Adapt as though your house is on fire, and the only way out is blocked. What will you do to adapt? Adapt as though you are on the Titanic, and there are no more life preservers or lifeboats. What will you do to adapt? Adapt as if your life depends on it. Why?

*Your life **does** depend on it.*

ACHIEVE

Once you look around and accept the reality of your life, you can adapt to the circumstances that you are currently facing. Once you begin adapting to and dealing with your current circumstances, you will slowly but surely, step-by-step, day-by-day, inch closer to your goal. Indeed, once you accept and adapt, you *will* achieve.

Yes, my great grades and upbringing soon gave way to drugs, alcohol, and a hostile attitude toward other people. My family was no longer a family, and I was no longer interested in making plans for my future. Ultimately, I dropped out of school. But after living in the "real world" for a while, I soon realized the value of education. I soon learned the value of a good attitude. More importantly, as I look back on that fateful day in the halls of Buena Vista High School, I learned that a bad attitude can ruin your whole life.

64: GETTING OUT

A bad attitude can lead to bad choices (like the decision to fight at a crowded basketball game; or the decision to start a fight just before school).

A bad attitude can affect how you see and feel about the world.

On the other hand, a good attitude can also affect how you see and feel about the world.

The cool thing is this: you can actually control your own attitude! In fact, your attitude is really the only attitude that you can really control.   However, many people simply "give" control of their attitude to other people and events.

But, after reading *Getting Out*, you will have the power to understand how to control and improve your attitude. After reading *Getting Out,* you will see just how easy it is to obtain and keep a positive attitude. In fact, after reading the next chapter of this book, you will see how easy it is to accept the simple premise of "attitude choice."   Moreover, you will understand how to adapt to this premise. And, yes, you will achieve an overwhelmingly positive attitude... simply by reading the next chapter.

Life is not a big game. But if it were, you would still be in control of your actions and attitudes.

Are you responsible for **your** actions?
What about **your** attitudes?
Who "makes" **you** mad?

The answer may surprise **you**
Read on...

ACCEPT   ADAPT   ACHIEVE ®

7: The Elevator of Life

So there I was... suspended for one calendar year from one high school while attending a school on the other side of town. I had accepted the reality of my situation, and I subsequently adapted and achieved a worthwhile solution.

However, I still had a bad attitude. And I did not adapt well to the significant cultural differences between my old and new environments. Ultimately, I elected to join the United States Navy after earning a high-school certificate via a General Equivalency Diploma (GED). Yes, I was one of the teenagers who wanted to "see the world." And over the course of a twenty-year career in the United States Navy, I saw a world far different than that of Mid-Michigan.

Think about this: I dropped out of school because I did not adapt well to the cultural differences of two very different schools. However, during my travels throughout the world, I experienced a fascinating planet, full of cultures, climates, and creatures wonderfully and beautifully different than my own. Ultimately, I learned to appreciate our respective differences.

ACCEPT   ADAPT   ACHIEVE ®

66: GETTING OUT

Over the years, I have lived in states from Hawaii to Virginia, and several cities in between. I have visited Guam, China, Korea, Japan, Mexico, Curacao, Germany, and Iraq.

As I moved from place to place, I met some very interesting people. Some of those people had some pretty bad attitudes. And some of those interesting people had good or great attitudes. After my arrival back in the United States, I dedicated a lot of time to reflecting on the differences in the attitudes of the people I had met. Why are some people positively minded? On the other hand, why do some people have a negative frame of mind? What determines the difference between a good attitude and a bad attitude?

Eventually, I began to understand the awesome power of personal choice: having a good or bad attitude is as simple as "deciding" to have one or the other. However, all too often, people simply *choose* to have a bad attitude.

I have seen countless examples where associates, friends, and strangers blame anyone and everything for a situation which was initially caused entirely by them. Unlike those blameless people, you should see the power of choice as a powerful tool that can be used to achieve your goals.

Unfortunately, many students see choices as "forks in the road," like the capital letter 'Y', where Choice A differs *slightly* from Choice B. Actually, choices are more like a 'T' in your path... not so much a *slightly* different route, but rather a **totally** different path altogether, completely opposite in direction and principle than the other available journey.

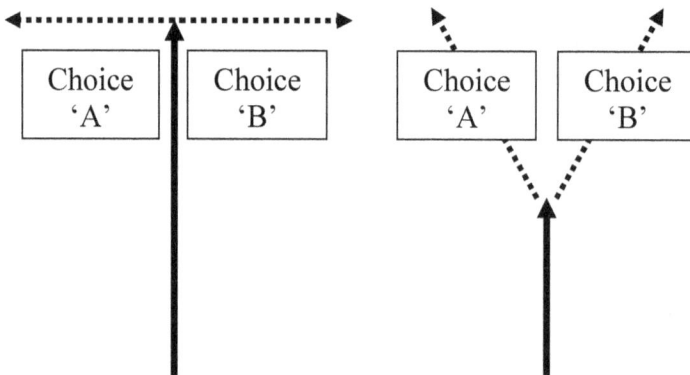

Paths and perceived choices

ACCEPT ADAPT ACHIEVE ®

But how can you recognize and navigate the many different choices you face every day? How can you make sure you are making the right decision when selecting from multiple paths, journeys, and routes? How can you keep an alert mindset to keep from believing your life has lost a certain amount of meaning?

You certainly can't go around quoting songs like, "Be Happy"! People would probably get tired of seeing you come around. And to be sure, on some days, it seems like everything is truly going wrong. Perhaps you missed your ride to school, got a bad grade report, or simply got into an argument with one of your friends. On those days, it can be hard to keep a good attitude; however...

I am asking you to consider the similarities between your life and the simple mode of transportation called

The Elevator

In this vast world of souls, our lives are forever flowing into and out of one building and into the next... from one structure to another, in a sea of schools, houses, towers, shops, malls, and associated dwellings. Within all of these buildings, our lives and minds travel in and out of the various structures without a great deal of thought about how we get from Point A to Point B. We arrive at our destination, literally and figuratively, without significant forethought.

68: GETTING OUT

Many girls awake in the morning and decide what to wear. They choose a skirt, blouse, or jeans. And, as you know, many teenagers like to wear makeup. Ask five girls why they wear makeup, and you will probably get five different answers. But, in general, girls (and women) wear makeup to enhance their already existing physical beauty. Some girls wear a lot of makeup; others wear just a little bit. But here is my main point: every one of these girls makes a choice about wearing makeup. Every one of those girls choose if, when, and how much makeup to wear.

Moreover, their decision to wear makeup affects how other people see them. That's right: girls (and women) wear makeup, and it changes how the world sees them.

You should do the same thing with your attitude.

You should take some time at the beginning of your day and decide how you want other people to view you. Your appearance is made up of clothes, jewelry, hair, skin tone, and several other characteristics. But your attitude also plays a very big part of your interaction with other people.

Students everywhere awake in the morning and set a course for school. As you probably know, students typically don't spend much time thinking about how they will get to school. They usually arrive at the school the same way they did yesterday and the day before that. And immediately after arriving at school, they go to their first classroom, and then start socializing or learning... never really giving much thought to their attitude and how it affects their appearance and interaction with others.

The "Elevator of Your Mind" concept is an example of how you can set aside some time before you start the day and actually *decide* to have a positive attitude throughout the day.

ACCEPT   ADAPT   ACHIEVE ®

And if you can set a course of positive thought and action for one specific day, you can probably put together six or seven straight days of positive thought... and end up with a whole week's worth of great, positive decision-making.

A positive attitude is actually a very valuable gift that only you can give to yourself. No one else can do for you what you have the power of doing with your attitude. No one else can give you your attitude. Moreover, no one else can give you a bad attitude. It's entirely up to you!

I'll say it again: if you can start your day with *one* good thought, followed by one good choice, and another good thought and good choice, you can set forth a fundamentally positive day. That positive day can actually be connected to another successfully positive day... and then another... until, before you know it, your week has been a smashing success!

And, if you can put this process in practice for a day and a week, you can put this process in place for two, three, and four weeks. In other words, if you can do this for one day; you can do it for seven days (a week). If you can do it for a week, you can do it for four weeks (a month).

And, if you can do it for a month... you can do it for a year. If you follow this process for a year... it will become part of who you are. Indeed, it will define who you are: you will be a positive person with a *great* attitude.

Like the physical elevator you can see in every tall building, the Elevator of Your Mind starts with one simple choice. As you stand before the closed doors of the yet-to-be-called elevator, you are faced with one sole, simple choice: up or down? Quite simply...

Which button will **YOU** press?

~ Up or Down? ~

If you press the "up" button, the elevator will take you up. If you press the "down" button, the elevator will certainly take you down. And in your very own life, "turning on" a good or bad attitude is as simple as pushing a small button.

However, on too many occasions, people blame others for their attitude. People blame friends, family members, and enemies for *making* them mad. Some students even blame their teacher for *making* them lose their temper. Some students with jobs blame their jobs for *making* them unhappy. Yes, people blame, blame, and they blame. Why do people freely give so much blame to others?

Instead of *giving* the blame to others, we need to accept our respective roles in pressing the single button that raises or lowers the Elevator of Our Minds. We certainly don't blame other people when we get off at the wrong floor of an office building! We don't blame other people if we push the "down" button when we actually want to go *up* to a higher floor in an office building! Accordingly, we should not *ever* blame other people for our personal attitudes.

Like the physical elevator in a building, in the Elevator of Your Mind, regardless of how you arrived at your current place in life, you have to make a simple choice: *To what location will you go from here*? Yes, we all face challenges. Some of your day-to-day challenges may seem hopelessly insurmountable.

Indeed, some challenges appear impossible to overcome. However, as you stand in your respective box (elevator), you are faced with one critical choice: Will your thoughts and actions descend downward into the deep, darkest pit of despair? Or, will you press the "up" button and self-exalt yourself out of the current situation? It is entirely your choice. All you have to do is "press the 'up' button."

ACCEPT   ADAPT   ACHIEVE ®

Think about it: you can literally travel to any one of the floors in any of the buildings in any of the cities of the world. There are countless structures to enter, and there are many, many floors onto which you can enter. There are floors below you, and there are many levels above your current location. Every single one of those floors is *yours* for the asking.

*But **you** must start by pushing one simple button.*

Why is this one simple button so critical? Why do I stress the importance of this ultra-important single switch? I continue to accentuate the importance of this button because it does two very specific things.

First, the button concept puts **you** in control. No one can change your attitude except you. Oh, sure, other people can *influence* your emotions. But, ultimately, the choice to go up or down with your attitude is a personal choice; it is *your* very own specific, **unavoidable** decision.

> *You alone choose the direction of your attitude.*

Secondly, by pushing the button yourself... **you** cannot give blame to anyone. Instead, you must simply accept the ability to control and use your thoughts only in the most positive applications.

After entering the Elevator of Your Mind, you will face a multitude of additional choices. There are several floors onto which you can go; some floors are above you; some floors are below you; and you can always come back to the same floor. Regardless of the available choices, the decision is yours. Think about where you want to go in life; then head in that specific direction. You may find immediate success.

Or, you may acquire a vast wealth of unrelated experiences along the way. Regardless of the direct or meandering route of your path, remember: it *is* your path. Accordingly, do not subscribe to the theory of blame. Your path is chosen by you and you alone.

You are who you are. But, then again, you can be who you can be. We all have an inner core of self. For the most part, this sense of self is changeless. Most people would agree that the person they are today is not significantly different than the person they were "a while back." In general, this is a true statement.

However, since we are an aggregate sum of our respective experiences, one particular experience can have a fantastically strong effect on our lives. This effect can be negative or positive. This effect, in and of itself, does not have to be of particular importance to anyone else.

In other words...you and only you...
provide the relative importance for an experience.

If something is important to you; it is important to you because you make it important to you. For example, if you like chocolate ice cream, you will probably make it important to have chocolate ice cream in your house. However, chocolate ice cream is not necessarily my favorite ice cream. Therefore, the relative importance (of chocolate ice cream) to me is very small when compared to the importance you might place on it. Thus, I will probably not keep chocolate ice cream in my house.

Likewise, some people think "street respect" is important. Others don't really care about street respect. Some people say "grades are important." Other people may say, "Just try your best."

The level of importance is determined by individuals.

However, when individuals become a collective unit (like Congress or a school board), individuals often translate their ideas, concepts, likes, and wishes onto the whole group of individuals.

What are some important things to you? Do you value street cred? Do you value family? Is money your greatest concern? Is a nice car important to you? What about friends... are they important? If friends are important, how important are they?

In addition to family members and friends... the books you read, the television shows you watch, and the classes in which you learn all help form the person that is you. All of those influences shape your idea of what is important. All of those influences eventually become a major part of who you are as a person.

The previously read chapters of this book are now part of who you are. Please share the wisdom herein. Loan or give this book; speak these truths; and help your friends change the way they currently think.

You are already a changed person.

Figure 1: No Negativity, please!

Stay focused on being a positive-minded person. Minimizing negativity may seem like a gargantuan challenge in the media-rich culture we currently live. However, in the following chapters, I will introduce a few concepts and tools to help you constructively navigate the challenges presented by negative people, places, and events. The best way to refute negativity is to be positive.

Engage other people. *Share* your positive energy. The more you share your anti-negative sentiment, the greater the confidence you will have to continuously seek and select your chosen direction: using the "up" button.

ACCEPT   ADAPT   ACHIEVE ®

74: GETTING OUT

Sometimes, you will exit the Elevator of Your Mind onto the "wrong floor." Simply turn around, find the Elevator call button, and get back on your specific Elevator. But first, you must choose to go "up." There is *always* a choice to be made.

If you have had the opportunity to explore the "wrong floor"; learn from the experience. If your previous choices seem to have impacted your life in a negative manner, consider what has happened; learn from the events; and then move on to bigger and better things. Moving on to more important things is a choice that **must** be made. Stop mentally laboring over past experiences. Get over it!

In fact, simply forget about it! Once you have acquired the lessons from your learning experiences, allow those experiences to float to the back of your mind. The mind has an incredible ability to remember almost everything you have ever experienced (recall is usually the difficult part). Accordingly, don't worry or wonder if you have learned what you were *supposed* to learn.

Forgive yourself; forgive others; and then move on. We have all made mistakes; no one is perfect. And, guess what: from this point forward, no one will ever **be** perfect. You and I both will make many more mistakes in our lives.

As you very well **know**... the person you see in the mirror will occasionally fumble the ball or drop the glass. I am not perfect, and neither are you. Thus, you should not expect *other* people to perform flawlessly in their respective lives. Other people will also make many more mistakes.

And, as an imperfect person yourself, you should certainly expect to forgive other people when they *push your (elevator) buttons.*

However...
*You are now the **only** one pushing your Elevator buttons.*

Life is painfully simple. We are born, we live, and then we die. In between, each of us has the undeniable ability to create our very own personal paradise; as a matter of choice...

ACCEPT   ADAPT   ACHIEVE ®

...we also have the distinct ability to create our very own nightmare. In the following chapters, I will present a very simple and direct path to creating and keeping only the personal paradise... the place *you* have the ability to achieve.

You are now ready to open the door to your future...

You now understand the steps to
Getting Out
of your situation...

...no matter what the situation is!

8: Take Your Time

Once you become a high school senior, you have successfully managed to navigate your way through the newness of the freshman year; the changes faced during sophomore year; and, yes, the second-place finish of last-year's junior year. But what do you do next? Where do you go from here?

Of course, over the previous three years, you have been preparing for this last year of high school. So much in your life has changed in those three short years. Perhaps you have learned how to drive; maybe you have a driver's license. Perhaps you have acquired many new friends, while losing other close friends because of a geographic move across town or across the country.

Some events are more memorable than other events. Perhaps you have a favorite memory regarding a sporting activity; maybe something spectacular happened in your class, at your locker, or in your neighborhood.

Believe it or not... all those memories and all those events will work together to help prepare you for life after high school. A team sport helps us get along well with others... not just on the field, but off the field as well. Having your own locker teaches you responsibility for keeping your valuables safe, as well as respecting the personal space of others. Of course, learning how to drive a car is a skill that will continue to serve you long after you depart the halls of homeroom, hall monitors, and home-field advantage.

Preparation for life doesn't stop after you graduate. In fact, as we go through life, we should prepare ourselves in every way possible for the yet-to-come life ahead. In reality, our entire existence is spent preparing for some type of eventuality.

Proper diet and regular exercise help to prepare your body for the challenges of life. A proper diet gives your immune system the nutrients and fuel it needs to fend off attacks from viruses and bacteria. Your immune system is further boosted when you regularly exercise. In fact, habitual exercise actually changes the physical composition of your body. Through regular exercise, you will literally get better, stronger, and faster. With regular exercise, you will become better prepared to take on the challenges of life.

In general, the successes *and failures* of today will prepare you for the challenges of tomorrow. That's right: your **failures** or, as I like to say, your "learning lessons" will actually teach and help prepare you for bigger lessons in life. A "learning lesson" is not really a mistake... unless you don't take the time to learn from it.

Everyone faces failure at some point in life. But, like Thomas Edison, the inventor of the light bulb who failed several hundred times until he got it right... you and your failures are not what matters. You, your learning lessons, and your persistence are what matter most; those things will prepare you for life.

And, in a very similar fashion, this chapter can help prepare you for a successful life after high school. Like a steady diet of delicious fruits, tasty vegetables, and lean meat, a careful study of the next few pages can make all the difference in your world... and the world of your children whom you may someday have to support.

Yes, I realize that having and supporting children may actually be (literally) the last thing on your mind right now. However, at some point in life, you will probably start a family. At some point in life after high school, you will seek the company and companionship of a cute boy (if you are a girl), or a lovely lady (if you are a guy).

And, as you probably already know... guys and girls are the initial beginnings of a family. Believe me: when I was a Senior in high school, I would never have guessed that, twenty years later, I would have three daughters... giggling little girls looking to me, their father who used to be a Senior at Buena Vista High School.

And, yes... you, too, will someday lead the life of a young one. Regardless of whether your children will be born next week or within the next five years, the best time to prepare for that event is *today*. Because, just like the 8th grade prepared you for the 9th grade; and just like the 10th and 11th grades prepared you for senior year, the next few years of your life will significantly affect how you spend the later years of your life.

Just think: in three short years, you will probably be twenty-one years old. Just three short years ago, you were learning the ropes of high school. How much more is there to learn about life?

Remember when you were nine years old and couldn't wait to be (the double-digit) ten years old? Well, if you don't remember back that far, perhaps you can remember what it was like to be twelve years old... and waiting impatiently to become that wonderful TEENager.

But wait: after turning thirteen, most new teenagers immediately start looking forward to fifteen and sixteen. After all, no one really wants to be a "new" teenager, right?

And, ahhhhh, yes... Then there is the sixteen-year-old student who simply can't wait to be eighteen glorious years old. Indeed, there is something special and seemingly magical about turning eighteen.

More accurately...

*There is something more **legal** about turning eighteen.*

Yes, as an eighteen-year-old student, you are a legal adult in the "eyes of the law." Of course, this can be a good thing... or a bad thing, depending on if you are a good eighteen-year-old student or a bad eighteen-year-old student.

Interestingly, many just-turned-eighteen-year-old men and women soon bore of being a "new" eighteen-year-old, and they simply cannot wait to be a "real" adult; a twenty-one-year-old man or woman. Most amusingly, by the time people reach the age of twenty-one, many have the same mentality, and they can't wait to be an "older" adult... something like a cool twenty-two or twenty-three-year-old guy or gal.

But then... all of a sudden, that twenty-two year-old gal soon realizes that the next stop is twenty-five; and then thirty! Oh no... all of a sudden, after being thirty, people start looking at ten-year blocks of time. That's right, after people cross the age of thirty, they soon see the "Big Four-O" standing in their path.

And... "just like that," our lives go from a nine-year-old kid who can't wait to be ten... all the way to a forty-year-old adult who can't seem to remember where all the time went. So... what's my point?

My point is this: *enjoy your youth.*

Your youth is the one treasure that you can never, ever get back. You will never see sixteen candles on a cake again... unless that same cake also has several more candles on it (in addition to the sixteen fire sticks). Likewise, you will never graduate from high school again. Oh, sure... you may have other graduations, but high school is where many of your life-long friendships are formed. High school is where you grew up. High school is where you learned algebra. High school is where you did a lot of "firsts." Perhaps you had your first crush, kiss, or concern of a person of the opposite sex.

Perhaps you obtained your first driver's license. Perhaps you went to your first dance, date, or daytime party. No matter where you go or what you do, you will always have the memory of high school and the things you did there first.

So, enjoy your youth! Spend time with friends, family, and folks you barely know. Over the years spent in high school, your life will change dramatically. Remember: after high school, there are no more Homerooms. There is no more recess. There are no more tardy slips or parental excuses.

After high school, **you** set the pace. *You* ring the bell. *You* make the plan. Accordingly, **you** must *accept* the full responsibility and accountability of your life. The choices you face today, and the decisions you make tomorrow will have a significant impact on the rest of your life.

So in the following chapters, we will review a detailed plan to help you decide what's best for your specific life. Indeed, not everyone will decide to go to college. Some people feel "all schooled out" and want to immediately join the workforce. Others may want to travel far away and truly see the world. Still others will want to serve humanity and address the simple needs of others. The following chapters will address each of these preferences. And, by the time you are finished reading this book, you will have a better understanding of the range of opportunities available to you.

By the time you finish reading this book, you will be much more prepared to face life after high school. By the time you finish reading this book, you will have a plan for achieving a successful life.

By the time you finish reading this book,
you will have a real-life plan for *Getting Out*.

9: If...

In life, we are where we are. There is no yesterday or tomorrow. Thus the biggest question is: where are you?

Mentally, are you ready to make it on your own?

Physically, are you prepared to deal with the challenges of a life without the guidance of parents, teachers, and hall monitors? Financially, are you equipped to deal with the very real responsibilities of rent, groceries, transportation, insurance, clothes, toiletries, and, perhaps gifts?

In reality, no one is every really prepared to deal with all of these things. No teenager ever leaves school with all the right education, knowledge, and understanding. In truth, everyone (yes, everyone) continues to learn long after graduating from high school. Sometimes, the continued education is in the form of college and graduate school. For others, the workplace will teach them quite a few things about life, people, and living with people.

Unfortunately, there is no single book that can provide all the answers to all of your questions. However, the last few chapters of this book will help prepare you for the college application process. And there are also a few tidbits of information for those bright, industrious students who simply want to see the world or go straight into the workforce.

~ Almost There ~

Well, here you are... almost finished with this book. Take a moment and flip back to the Introduction of this book. On Page xiv of this book, I state the following:

> *My goal for you is simple: finish reading this book.*
>
> *If you can finish reading this book, and if you can follow the simple advice in the final chapters, you will certainly succeed at achieving two very important things:*
>
> *1. You will achieve a simple goal of finishing this book;*
> *2. You will understand preparation for adulthood.*

Over the last 80 pages, I have provided a few key insights into some very basic truths about life. I have also shared my experience as a student and young man. At this point in the book, you have basically achieved the one main goal I established for you on page xiv. You have essentially finished the book. For achieving that goal, you are now rewarded with an increased level of knowledge. The information you have gained from reading the previous pages is now forever in your mind. No one can ever take that away from you!

Of course, you may say to yourself, "But I don't really remember all the stuff I read in all the other chapters of *Getting Out*." Well... that's okay. It's okay because, as a matter of scientific fact, your brain remembers everything. The human brain is like a very powerful computer; and it has the power never to forget. The tough part is usually "recalling" the information that is stored in your brain.

So... to help you recall the information you previously read in this book, here is a quick review:

- In the Introduction, I explained *Why I Wrote This Book*.

- In Chapter 1, I opened up my past and told you *My Story*.

- In Chapter 2, I discussed some thoughts on *Our Story*.

- In Chapter 3, I revealed *The Big Three*.

- In Chapter 4, I exposed *The Bitter Taste of Revenge*.

- In Chapter 5, I introduced *The Other Big Three*.

- In Chapter 6, we reviewed *The Power of Denial*.

- In Chapter 7, I shared the allegory of *The Elevator of Life*.

- In Chapter 8, I advised you to *Take Your Time*.

And here we are at Chapter 9. As you may have noted, the title of this chapter is simply "IF..." The word "IF" is such a small, tiny physical word. Yet, the word "IF" can affect your life in some very substantial, huge ways.

If, for example, you had never been born, you would not be here. Now, that may seem like a simple or extreme use of the word "IF..." However, that is a correct statement.

> *If you had not started reading this book,*
> *you would not have finished this book.*

ACCEPT   ADAPT   ACHIEVE ®

Again, these examples may appear simple, but they are nevertheless true. You can't finish what you have never started. You certainly can start whatever it is that you want to start, and you can choose to finish whatever it is that that have started.

So, the only question is: what do you want to start?

Indeed, your high-school career is concluding. You will soon be finished with all those years of bells, quizzes, tests, and teachers. Or will you?

In reality, we never stop learning.

If you decide to get a new job after high school, you will learn new responsibilities, innovative ideas, and different skills. If you decide to attend more school via college, you will learn new theories, new languages, and different cultures. If you decide to sit at home and watch television, you will learn how to recite new commercials, new shows, and different videos and songs.

If you decide to join the military or other service organization, you will learn personal accountability (being responsible for your actions), professional demeanor (how to present yourself in a purposeful manner), practical skills (ability you can learn in the military, but also use as a civilian).

Interestingly, take a look back at the two previous paragraphs, and you will see two very important words repeated throughout the lines of words... Those two very powerful words are...

1. If

2. Decide

Yes... you now have all the power in the world. You can change your life forever by understanding and accepting the power of your personal choice in life. YOU have the power to decide what to do with your life. YOU have the power to choose between getting a job, going to college, joining the military... or anything else in the *whole wide world*.

YOU have the power to choose how YOUR life will be spent. And the best part about this great choice is this: you can always change your mind if you don't like your first choice! That's right... if you decide to get a job tomorrow, but later decide to go to college, that's quite okay. Similarly, if you think college is the best option (and it is), but decide later that you really want to join the military... you can do that, too!

In other words, you don't have to have everything "all figured out" by the time you finish reading this book!

However, you simply must understand and accept the power of the responsibility *you* have when making personal choices in *your* life. You are the boss of you and your life. Sure, there are parents, family members, and real-life bosses to whom you must pay attention. However, in the final analysis, you will ALWAYS do what you decide to do.

Notice I did not say, "You will do what you want to do."

I specifically stated, "You will ALWAYS do what you decide to do." This is true because, no matter what happens, you are responsible and accountable for your own actions. Indeed, other people can influence your decision. But, in the end, you tell your arms and legs what to do. You make the ultimate decision of campus life, military life, or simply living life with a job and benefits.

Think back over your years in middle school and high school. Perhaps you were influenced a time or two by your friends (the technical term for this is "peer pressure"). Perhaps you really wanted to do "the right thing," but you ended up doing something you should not have done. Who can you blame for your actions? Was it your friends' fault that you didn't do the right thing? Or, more correctly, was it your fault for not choosing the right decision?

Indeed, you will ALWAYS do what *you* decide to do.

Others may influence you... but your decisions are yours alone to make. Fortunately, this is true for good and bad outcomes. If you choose to go to college, upon college graduation, you can pat yourself on the back and say, "It was my decision to attend and complete college." If you join the military and move to some big city by the sea, meet your dream date, and live happily ever after, you can someday say, "I made the correct choice to join the military."

Indeed, you will ALWAYS do what *you* decide to do.

So the only question that remains is...what do you want to do? What do you want to do with your life... right here, right now? The choice is yours...

But what choices do you really have?

Education: Knowledge is an asset that can never be taken from you. Learning about new people, places, and things you will continue to do for the rest of your life. A formal education usually leads to increased earnings and an overall higher quality of life.

Economics: We all need food, clothing, & shelter. Stable earnings offer consistent access to good food, great clothes, and a very nice place to live. However, the ability to make *more* money is often tied to an increased level of skills, knowledge, and/or capabilities.

Opportunity: Success doesn't happen by mere chance. Success is 1% luck and 99% hard work. And work often prepares you for big opportunities when you least expect them. A good education will prepare you for the opportunity to improve your economic situation.

~ Choices ~

Today marks the beginning of your plan for *Getting Out.*

As discussed in Chapter 7, "*The Elevator of Life*," regardless of your current situation, you have the power to choose a good (or bad) attitude. Regardless of what happened yesterday, today is a day you can spend planning for a way out of your current situation.

Please don't underestimate the simplicity or bold truth about the Elevator of Life. Some people may say it's "too simplistic" or that it doesn't account for the realities of life. To those people I say one thing: we all choose how to react and respond to our situations; when we respond with a positive action plan, we learn to accept, adapt, and achieve success over the situation... instead of allowing the situation to have a greater influence or control over us.

Many students are confronted with very challenging situations. Teenage girls (and the responsible father) are sometimes facing an unplanned pregnancy. Some students are raised in an environment of illicit drug use and violent alcoholic families. Still other young people are victims of emotional, physical, or mental abuse. All of these situations can overwhelm some of the smartest, strongest people.

On the other hand, no matter what the situation, people can choose to acknowledge they do, in fact, need help, begin the process of change by seeking assistance, and ultimately accomplish a way out of their respective situation.

The same is true for you.

No matter what your circumstances...

1. You can choose to acknowledge your need for help.
2. You can change by seeking assistance, and...
3. You can accomplish a way out of your situation.

ACCEPT   ADAPT   ACHIEVE ®

Review those three previous statements:

> 1. You can choose to *acknowledge* your need for help.
> 2. You can *change* by seeking assistance, and...
> 3. You can *accomplish* a way out of your situation.

Did you notice the message inside of each statement? Here's a hint: look at the words on the bottom of every page in this book. Once you accept (acknowledge) the powerful concept of choice, you can begin to adapt (change) your life toward those things that can help you in a positive manner. After you have accepted and adapted to a new plan for your life, you can achieve (accomplish) anything!

In January 2009, Mr. Barack Obama became the 44th President of the United States of America. A few short years before his inauguration, President Obama was a freshman senator from Illinois. A few years before his election to the Senate in Illinois, he attended graduate school. A few years before graduate school, he studied to obtain a bachelor's degree. Before acquiring his bachelor's degree, Mr. Obama was a student in high school.

> You are a student in high school. You are a student of life.

Where will you be next year? Where will you be in five years? Where do you plan to be in ten years? Perhaps ten years seems like a long time from now; and maybe it is. After all, ten years ago, you were not even a teenager, right? On the other hand, what were you doing five years ago? Take a moment and think about the past 3-5 years of your life. What has happened over those years?

What has happened with your friends and family? What has happened in your school, your city, and your state? What has happened in the world? Most importantly, what has happened to YOU? Where have you been; where have you gone; what have you done?

As much as you have done in the last 3-5 years, there is so much more to do in the next year. There are so many more places to go in the next three years. And, yes, there is much that will happen to you in the next 3-5 years. You will continue to change. You will continue to learn (from other people, places, events, courses, classes, and trips).

So, the only question is: what do you want to start?

Education: You are now concluding at least 8 years of academic study. You have learned so much. But, then again, there is so much more to learn about this world!

Economics: As you get older, your ability to earn more money will be affected by your level of education, as well as your network of friends, family, and co-workers.

Opportunity: Unlike the picture of dice above, your life is not one big gamble. There are things you can do today to "hedge your bets" in a big way. Establish and maintain good relationships with everyone you meet... this is the initial process of increasing your network of contacts. Find and keep a good mentor. A good mentor can advise, listen, and challenge you to achieve greater goals. Moreover, a mentor might introduce you to his or her network; a valuable prize indeed!

~ Starting Anew ~

Now that you are finishing this book, my new goal for you is to accept your role as the leader of your life. You are the boss of you. You are the conductor of your own train in life. And yes... only YOU decide what to do with your life. Only you can decide **what** you want to do; **when** you want to start; and **where** you want to live your life. Only you can accept, adapt, and achieve the things you need to accept as you begin to adapt to the changes needed to achieve success in your life.

So, the only question is: what do you want to start?

The answer, it seems to me, should always be... "I want to start a successful life." Now this is a straightforward answer, but it is also very vague. It is a vague answer because only you can accurately state your definition of a "successful life." For some people, a successful life implies lots and lots of money. For others, a successful life depends on lots and lots of love. In reality, there is probably an unlimited number of ways to define "a successful life."

And, over time, like many people, your definition of a successful life will probably change.

When I was a student at Buena Vista High School in Saginaw, Michigan, the basketball team was very, very good. Actually, it was a *great* basketball team. In fact the BVHS boys' varsity basketball team went to the Michigan State Class B Championship Game in 1984 and 1985. Unfortunately, the team lost both games.

However, in 1986, the boy's basketball team went back to the State Championship Game for a third consecutive time. And, in this case, the third time was the charm. The Knights of Saginaw Buena Vista defeated Flint Beecher in a wild buzzer-beater of a game. With three seconds left on the clock, one of the Beecher players missed a free-throw attempt, and the ball was rebounded by Shaun Randolph, and tossed to Chris Coles at the top of the key. Chris launched what would become known as "The Shot." In one of the most shocking finals in the history of Michigan high school basketball, Chris launched a 55-foot three-pointer that landed softly through the net on the opposite end of the court... as the game clock expired.

The crowd went crazy! It was a highly unlikely shot. It was an unlikely ending. And it was an even unlikelier victory, considering the fact that the starting player for Buena Vista, Mark Macon, was out with an ankle injury.

Nevertheless, Chris will be forever remembered as the one who made "The Shot." Chris would go on to coach various basketball teams throughout the region, and Mark Macon, my neighbor from up the street went on to attend Temple University and eventually join the National Basketball Association and play for some pretty good teams.

And Saginaw Buena Vista would go on to hold a prominent spot in the record books of Michigan high school basketball. Coach Norwaine Reed and his teams took home four state trophies between 1986 and 1993.

Despite the consecutive state championship losses in 1984 and 1985, the legacy of young men coming through the basketball program at Saginaw Buena Vista understood the value of an ability to accept, adapt, and achieve.

They accepted the value of teamwork
They adapted and utilized the power of the true team.
They achieved a state championship.
(www.mhsaa.com)

Here's a question: when your opportunity knocks, what will you do? When you have the chance to make a once-in-a-lifetime shot at staying in school, will you be ready?

ACCEPT   ADAPT   ACHIEVE ®

You, too, can achieve your highest measure of success.

The question is: how do you define your level of success? What will be *your* trophy in the years to come? Will you have a job, a career, or a certificate of graduation? Will you have a life, a love, and a lot of money? Take the time to start a plan.

Remember: a failure to plan is a plan to fail.

The answers depend entirely upon you!

So, the only question is: what do you want to start?

10: The Nuts & Bolts of *Getting Out*

Start with your options for *Getting Out*

Make a list of the things you know you want to do. Do you like to travel? Do you like to tinker with cars? Do you like working with people? What about your preferences? Do you prefer to work outside or inside? Are you a warm-weather person; or do you like to experience all four seasons? Are you extremely family oriented, or are you a loner who likes to strike out on your own? Are you a future doctor, business person, airline pilot, or flight attendant? What drives your inner sense of principles, power, and passion?

Continue defining your Goals for *Getting Out*

After you have taken considerable time to think about and compare your likes, dislikes, wishes, and dreams... take a pen and paper and write down your top five interests. Try to narrow the list into specific categories like college; working as a carpenter; driving a truck; joining the military; etc. Once you have completed this list of five specific end goals, select the top three items and make these your primary, secondary, and third-place goals. Focus on matching up your true, inner feelings and mindset with those three specific goals. Of those goals, which one tugs at your heart the most? Ask yourself this one key, critical question: Which goal can I spend the next three years working toward... every single day of my life... and feel good about it while reaching for that goal?

Create Your Action Plan for *Getting Out*

Of the three goals you specified above, select one definite goal and **accept** that particular goal as your one true goal. You are now ready to **adapt** your life to integrate the changes necessary to **achieve** this one specific goal. Your adjustment process may take some effort; but with a few small changes in your lifestyle, every subsequent action, attitude, and ability will soon come together and provide the vehicle, map, and fuel for you to sail smoothly along your current and future paths to success. *You can do this!*

ACCEPT   ADAPT   ACHIEVE ®

Something to think about...

You are a student of school

.

You are a student of life

.

Your life is about to change forever

.

Failure to plan is a plan for failure

.

This book is a teacher

.

This book is a plan

*This book is **YOUR** plan!*

As you wrap up the main part of *Getting Out*, here are a few thoughts to consider. These are what I call "actual factuals."

1. *I am a student.* High school was truly a great time in my life. I had my first girlfriend; my first job; my first thoughts about my future life. But beyond high school and, more importantly, I am a student of life. Over the years, I have learned so many different but equally important things in my life. This book represents only the tiniest fraction of what I have learned... or what you can expect as options in your current life. Bottom line: Listen to others (including me); be prepared to learn many things from many, many people. But, in the end, you are the student of your own life. Teach yourself well.

2. *As a student of life, you will never stop learning.* Like me, you are also a student of school. As I look back on high school, I remember a few feelings of fear, fate, and failure. Interestingly, I often had a fearful feeling that failure was my fate. But here I am today, a successful author with a bachelor of business degree and an MBA from a well-respected educational institution. Bottom line: fear means nothing, especially when you are the boss of your own life.

3. *Your life is about to change forever.* In actuality, every single day, your life changes forever. However, people often use this phrase as a negative statement. They say something like, "That accident changed my life forever." Or, they state, "Those grades changed my life forever." The bottom line: Change occurs every minute of every day; your goal is to plan for change; make it happen.

4. *Failure to plan is a plan for failure.* This is a powerful point that should help you understand the importance of setting good goals. There is an old saying, "If you don't know where you are going... sooner or later, you will get there." Of course, the obvious questions are: Where is "there"...? To *where* do you want to go? At what end do you want to be? Bottom line: Start planning your future now... and someday, one day... you can get there!

5. *What you do after high school is YOUR choice.* As I have clearly stated in the previous pages: this is YOUR life. You are the decision-maker in your life. You are the author of "The Book of Your Life." Accordingly, you can achieve whatever it is that your heart desires. The bottom line: What does your heart truly desire?

6. *Question*: What can you do? *Answer*: You can do almost anything. Do you want to go to college? If you want a college degree, do some research and make a plan to get there. Better yet, read the last four chapters of this book.

7. *Question*: What can you do? *Answer*: You can do almost anything. Do you want to go to work in a particular industry or job? Do some research and think about the following characteristics:
      i. *Knowledge; Skills; Abilities; OJT*
      ii. *Apprentice training*
      iii. *Research your likes; know your dislikes*
      iv. *Pay; Location (close to or far from home?)*

8. *Question*: What can you do? *Answer*: You can do almost anything. Do you want to join the Armed Services? Many of the services offer significant opportunities for real-world training (think computers, leadership, and management). Do some research (aside from talking to a recruiter), and decide which is right for you...

   • *The United States Navy, Air force, or Marines*

   Be forewarned, the Armed Services do not tolerate any type of drug use. Before I could join, I had to request and sign a waiver reflecting my remorse and subsequent resolve never to do illicit drugs again.

9. *Question*: What can you do right now? *Answer*: **If...** you have time to hang out with friends, you certainly have the time to find a mentor. Invest in your future by finding a good, educated mentor. A good mentor is someone who will guide, nurture, and inspire you... especially when you *need* it (which is usually when you don't *want* it!).

Finally, on the next few pages, I will allow you to peek once again into my personal life. On the following pages, you will find an e-mail I sent to my own daughter, Destiny, as she was wrapping up her senior year in college.   Perhaps like you, she was unsure of what to do, where to do it, or how to get there. Inasmuch as I have provided insight to you in this book, I have also provided her similar guidance and insight as she transitioned from middle school to high school to college.

And, like you and I, my daughter is a student of life.

However, in this particular case, I am a student **and** a teacher. As a parent, leader, and author, I have an awesome power to shape and affect the lives of many, many people. My advice, when taken to heart, can change the course of your life. Instead of going to the Peace Corps, perhaps you decide to become a doctor... and **then** go to the Peace Corps. Instead of joining the military, perhaps you decide to go to college, and **then** offer your service to our country.

In either case, I have to be very careful with what I write within the covers of this book. And, at the very least, I should give you advice only if I am comfortable giving the same advice to my daughters. Believe me... I care greatly about my four daughters, and I would never give them any bad advice.

As the father of a daughter, I want the best possible life that she can have. I want to teach her the things that I think she needs to know. In addition to *my* thoughts, dreams, and plans for her life, I also want her to become an independent thinker who can plan, prepare, and succeed on the strength of her own thoughts, dreams, and plans... with or without any assistance or advice from me. My goal is to be her mindful mentor, her able advisor, and her greatest guidance counselor.

Over the previous years in her life, there were those times when my daughter didn't listen to my advice. But, then again, there were far more times when she *did* listen to and apply my advice.   And, though I'd like to take credit for her major achievements, in reality, she is due all the credit.

Thus, with great care and concern for you, the youth of today and the leaders of tomorrow, I offer you this small but significant slice of advice I gave to my daughter three months before her college graduation:

Dearest Destiny,

As the subject line of your e-mail says, "College is almost over..." But, more importantly, your independent life is just about to begin. Wow! What a fantastic part of your life's journey!!

As I look back on my collegiate years, I am amazed at how close those years seem to be (despite the long-ago timeline of my 1993 baccalaureate... sixteen years ago).

Yet, I am even more amazed at my travels, travails, and triumphs since departing from school. For me, school was a mere formality... something that the rest of the world "needed" to be able to believe in me. I have always believed in the Power of John.

For you, I see the same result. You now have a certification of creed from a major educational institution; this certification alone will form the basis for a positive real-world opinion about Destiny. The truth is... high schools and colleges are just proving grounds. You have proved (to the world and yourself) that you won't give up at an important task.

You have proved that you can truly learn new things. And, yes, you have proved that, despite your imperfect record, you are perfect when it counts.

The next question is... What ELSE do you want to prove to the world... and yourself (?)

Yes, your undergraduate college life is concluding... But in life, there is no clear-cut beginning or end... only landmarks along the way (of our respective journeys). And, as I have often tried to share: I am sometimes no smarter than you... merely a more seasoned traveler. Indeed, I am simply a little further down the road.

And, as such, I truly want you to avoid or at least be aware of the washed-out bridges, dangerous drivers, sunken roads, and other hazards to your safe journey forward.

I also want you to slow down and truly enjoy the view from where you currently sit.

I want you to enjoy the splendor of everything.

When you were seventeen years old, I wanted you to enjoy the life of a seventeen-year-old youth... not an eighteen or twenty-year-old. When you were nineteen years old, I wanted you to enjoy that frame of mind. And, yes, Destiny... my tune will never change. You are now a worried, lost, meandering soon-to-be college graduate.

ENJOY IT.

There is something quite magical about "not having it all figured out." In reality, none of us have it all figured out. Life is. That's right... Life IS (period). You can't define it; you can't manage it; and you certainly can't figure it out... until you have already lived that part of life you so desperately wanted to figure out.

What do I mean by all this psycho mumbo-jumbo? Well... there are some things that women will never know until they become a mother. And there are some things those same women-mothers will never see... unless and until they are grandmothers.

The same is true of the trajectory of boys, men, fathers, and grandfathers.

Likewise, the same is true for daughters, step-daughters, young ladies, and women... and college students like you. School is easy... you are taught, and then you are tested.

The experience of life can be a bit tougher; experience will test you first... and leave the questions for later. In truth, this is a good thing. Scary? Not really. Unknown? For sure!

But here is what else we know...

You have spent the last seventeen years of your life in school... learning by someone else's grade book, textbook, and "fact" book. Now it's time for you to experience YOUR book; the Book of Destiny. This, my dear daughter, is truly the grandest of books. YOU are the author, editor, and illustrator. YOU are the publisher, marketer, and distributor.

YOU are also a first-time author, editor, illustrator, publisher, marketer, and distributor. Thus, you simply MUST know this... you will be imperfect at the "first edition." We all are.

*Knowing that one simple, small, significantly superlative point will help you to relax and enjoy exactly where you are right now... You are a successful college graduate with a growing network of faithful friends, formal contacts, and feckless family members. YOU are the author, editor, illustrator, publisher, marketer, and distributor of the Book of Destiny. What **you** write upon your heart is what will be written upon **your** life.*

Write worry into your heart; and worry will be your Destiny.

Write confidence, conviction, and courage upon your heart... and there you will find your Destiny.

Write love, compassion, concern, and a genuine appreciation for the effort it takes to write a better second, third, & fourth edition of the Book of Destiny... and you'll be a best seller.

>> "Don't worry... you'll make it." <<

* How to Read the Appendices *

If you are reading this book early in your high-school career, take some time and carefully review the next four appendices. These last four chapters are a very specific blueprint for *Getting Out* of high school and into a good four-year college.

Of course, it's never too late to go to college, and you can always attend a local community college or night school. But if you have the time to invest in a good preparation plan, follow the format of the following College Application Plan, and you will be well on your way to a successful *college* career!

- If you are a freshman in school, start with Appendix 1.

- If you are a sophomore, read Appendix 1 and 2.

- If you are a junior, start with Appendix 3.

- If you are a senior in high school, let's go right to Appendix 4. But you should also read appendices 1-3.

The appendices provide step-by-step advice on how to best prepare for applying to a four-year college. If you accept the plans as they are, and begin to adapt to the changes suggested in each of them, you will very likely achieve the goal of attending a college or university.

Each appendix follows the same basic structure:
✓ Ten basic steps per plan;
✓ Reasons why you should follow my advice;
✓ What can happen if you don't follow my advice;
✓ "Something to think About"

Additionally, I have added a few "Most Important Points." These MIPs are designed to help you set a priority of "what's really important" as you go through the process of planning for, applying to, and preparing for college. *Read all of them.*

ACCEPT   ADAPT   ACHIEVE ®

GETTING OUT

Appendix 1: THE FRESHMAN PLAN

NOTES

ACCEPT   ADAPT   ACHIEVE ®

STEP 1:
Choose a Place to Keep Your Files

The next three years of your life will have a great impact on how you spend the next ten years of your life. And, believe it or not, your entire life can be affected by one simple application.

Think about this:

- MIP #1 -
Getting organized will save you time, money, and effort.

Why do this?

By keeping your information in one, central place, you will not lose anything. You will also quickly find exactly what you are looking for. Most important, though, is the fact that, over the next few years, your personal files will grow significantly. You will acquire a learners' permit and a driver's license; you will probably get a job; and you will also get numerous report cards. Paychecks and pay stubs will help you when the time comes to file taxes (yes... taxes!). These and other documents must be kept in a safe place. Choose your safe place today.

What can happen if you don't do this?

Many records and files can be easily reproduced, especially in the digital age that we live. However, if you lose your social security card, driver's license, or other important documents, getting a new one will cost you time and money... as well as the thought of someone else having your personal information.

Ask any senior and she will tell you...

"*Time soon passes all too quickly!*"

ACCEPT   ADAPT   ACHIEVE ®

STEP 2:
Establish and Grow Your Vision

What do you really want to do with your life? This is a tough question. Some people are well over the age of 30 before they "know" what they want to do. Relax; you have time to think.

Why do this?

When you actually take a few hours, days, or months to really think about what you want to do, sooner or later, you will automatically start looking for ways to achieve your innermost thoughts. And, after you have established a certain vision in your mind, you can begin looking for the paths to achieve your vision. Keep in mind: your vision is not set in stone. You can change your destination at any time. Remember: failure to plan is actually a plan to fail. As a teenager, you have almost your whole life ahead of you. Create and plan a vision today!

What can happen if you don't do this?

It has been said that, "if you don't know where you are going, sooner or later you will get there." Where is "there"? If you don't set your sights on a specific goal, you may end up letting others make important choices and decisions for you instead of with you. If that happens, you have no one to blame except yourself.

Think about this...

You have changed so much since you first arrived at middle school two years ago.

Imagine the many changes that will occur over the next two years, up until you become a high-school junior.

Imagine! Dream!

Like an architect who is building his own life, see your future in your mind first.

Then create your vision.

ACCEPT   ADAPT   ACHIEVE ®

STEP 3:
Share Your Vision

A vision is simply a thought that you or someone else has placed in your mind. Once you write that vision down, it becomes a plan. By sharing your plan, you show a sincere belief in your plan.

Why do this?

When you share your vision, you are starting the process of bringing your vision into existence. Moreover, you will begin to assess how you really feel about your personal vision. When you share your vision, some people will be glad to hear about your future, and some may even offer help. Others, however, may challenge your beliefs. Others may dispute your ideas and dreams. Some people may even laugh at your dreams. If they do laugh at you or your dreams, simply use their laughter as fuel for your vision engine. Use their doubt to refine your dreams.

What can happen if you don't do this?

You can share your vision in many different ways. Write it down; give an oral presentation; tell family members. The point is: tell *somebody*. Perhaps they will actually help you achieve your vision. However, if you don't tell anyone, you may risk having a great-but-untested vision. Worse yet, you may risk losing or forgetting the idea.

Think about this:

Every great invention or work of art originated in the mind of its original creator.

Every high school freshman has a goal and vision of graduation.

Keep going...

Dream of your college graduation!

Sharing your vision of going to college can result in someone actually helping you get there!

STEP 4:
Get an SAT/ACT Study Book

The SAT and ACT are the standards by which you will be judged. You don't necessarily have to do well on these tests; but you simply must take one of these two tests. Start studying today!

Think about this:

If you start studying for these tests today, you will be an expert by the time you are a junior.

Why do this?

According to The College Board, over two million students take the SAT® annually; almost every college in the USA accepts the SAT or Subject Tests as an integral part of their admissions process. The ACT® test will test YOUR overall educational development, as well as your ability to do college-level work. Don't look at these tests as "just another test." Colleges use these tests to determine admittance criteria. Some schools may use the results of the tests to determine the amount of scholarship money you receive. So ask yourself, "How much $$ do I want?"

Start an easy habit: study your booklets for about 30 minutes every night... That's a whopping 210 minutes each week (3.5 hours a week!)

Get your SAT® or ACT® study book today!

What can happen if you don't do this?

Like high-school tests, if you study for the SAT/ACT, you will do better. If you don't study for the tests, you will not perform very well on the tests, and this will affect how school administrators view your record. Please remember: administrators are looking at your *official record*; they are not looking at you. How do you want to be viewed?

Knowledge is a gift to yourself.

STEP 5:
Daydream

Stop! Go! Don't do this! Don't do that! Wouldn't it be great if you could forget about all the rules that exist? If you could do anything and go anywhere, what and where would it be?

Why do this?

When you dream, you pay attention to "what could be." When you dream, you don't concern yourself about what other people think. Dreaming is all about **your** thoughts. Dreaming is all about a different reality. Dreaming is all about the reality in your mind. Does this reality actually exist? Of course it does... you just have to bring that reality into the view of other people. But first, you must take the easiest step: dream. What will you do? Where will you go? Don't worry about how you will get there. Don't worry about what it may cost. Just dream!

What can happen if you don't do this?

If you stop dreaming, you may stop believing in the limitless possibilities of your future. If you don't dream, you may limit your access to only things that can be seen with your eyes. But if a blind man can go to college, you can too! If a poor girl can graduate from a university, you can too! Believe in your dreams; not just your eyes. Dream!

Think about this:

A dream is free; it will cost you only a thought or two.

A single thought, when transformed into reality, can be worth millions of dollars.

Think of your dreams as a plan for your next life.

Your dreams are a very real part of your life.

Your life is the result of your innermost dreams.

ACCEPT   ADAPT   ACHIEVE ®

STEP 6:
Know Your Guidance Counselor

Next to your parents, your Guidance Counselor can have the greatest impact on your life. Accordingly, you should spend lots (and lots) of time getting to know your Guidance Counselor!

Why do this?

Literally thousands of students have graduated from your high school before you. And, by the time you graduate high school in a few short years, many more students will have put on the cap and gown... and moved on to college. Many of those students will come back to visit their old Guidance Counselor. Of course, their former Guidance Counselor is probably your current Guidance Counselor. When those current college students come back to visit, they tell their "old" Guidance Counselor what worked, what didn't work, and what worked really well.

What can happen if you don't do this?

If you don't get to know your Guidance Counselor early in your high-school career, you may miss out on valuable information and programs. He or she may have additional information on *Getting Out* of your current environment. He or she may also know of a current college student who is willing to help you chart your course.

Think about this:

- MIP #2 -

Aside from you, your Guidance Counselor is the most important person at your school.

In life, we all have our own path. But some roads have already been travelled.

Seek a lesson from someone who has already been there.

STEP 7:
Plan to Play Team Sports

Many colleges want to see how well you get along with other students. Your participation in team sports is a good indicator of this, and is also a great way to *learn* how to "play with others."

Why do this?

An athletic scholarship is a great way to achieve a college degree. However, in reality, only a small percentage of scholarships are based on athletic ability. Your participation in team sports reflects a friendly competitive nature, as well as a good introduction to effective time-management skills. Moreover, an active lifestyle will help you blow off a little stress that can sneak up on you during mid-terms and final exams during high school. After getting involved in high-school team sports, you can add the phrase "team player" to your college application.

What can happen if you don't do this?

By passing up the opportunity to play team sports, you will miss out on the fantastic fun and thrill of victory. More importantly, college administrators and scholarship committees will soon judge your official record and application against the applications of other high-school students, all of whom are competing for cash and college.

Think about this:

Team sports teach the rules of the sport. But they also teach the value of teamwork, camaraderie, and how to lose gracefully.

*Colleges are looking for people who are great winners as well as those who can **accept** defeat when bested by a better opponent.*

This is a metaphor for life.

Life is not a big game...

...but if it were, I'd like to learn and know the rules.

STEP 8:
Accept and Understand Your Role

Know that the most important person in the whole world is **you**. You must absolutely, positively believe this. Yes, there are other important people. But without you, there could be no "you."

Why do this?

When you graduate from high school and go to college, you will begin to experience more freedom. Indeed, by the time you graduate high school, you will be a young lady or a young man. Wow... that's pretty cool. But here's something to consider: you are also expected to be more responsible for yourself, your actions, and your **re**actions. Over the next few years of high school, if you miss the bus, skip a class, or fail a test, you have no one else to blame except your "self." You and your actions are controlled by you. *Take* responsibility; never *give* blame.

What can happen if you don't do this?

If you don't accept the role of a responsible young adult, you may look for ways to blame others, instead of seeking smart solutions for your own challenges. You are the leader of your own life; you are also the follower of your own life leadership. Learn how to accept your responsibilities. Someday, you will lead more than just yourself.

Think about this:

You are in the best possible position to prepare for college.

From the beginning of your freshman year, you have over 36 months to plan for graduation.

By accepting the role of "Most Important Person," you will learn to do all that you can do to make your education a success.

Accept the gift of time and use it wisely!

Spend your time achieving your dreams.

ACCEPT   ADAPT   ACHIEVE ®

STEP 9:
Plan to Get a Job

Working with others, like participation in team sports, can teach you things about life. Some subjects, like math, are very formal. Other lessons are more like on-the-job-training (OJT).

Why do this?

Maybe you will go to college; maybe you won't. However, chances are, someday you *will* have a job. And, in reality, you already have a job: your job is to learn all that you can while you are in school. You are learning how to write well, make sense of math, and, perhaps, how to best use the computer and Internet. But you are also learning how to follow rules; how to engage in adult conversation; and how to prepare for your next year in high school (you learn this from the upper classmen). Well, the next logical step is to learn in the "real world."

What can happen if you don't do this?

When you offer your assistance, you give a part of yourself. When you get a job and begin receiving paychecks, you will soon learn the value of money. If you don't have any experience with working or volunteering, your college application may not compete well with other student applications. Remember: college boards look for team players.

Think about this:

College applications are free. However, when you submit the application (online or via snail mail), most colleges require an application fee.

A job can help prepare for other college-related expenses.

A job is not just work;

...it's also a social playground.

ACCEPT   ADAPT   ACHIEVE ®

STEP 10:
Get to Know Your High School

Whether you are in middle school or at a full-scale high school, as a 9th grader, you are entering a whole new world. Invest some time getting to know all that you can about your high school.

Why do this?

Just three short years ago, you were a little kid in the sixth grade. Likewise, three short years from now, you will, again, shift teenage gears and become a young adult. Essentially, over the next three years, you will "grow up." Accordingly, you should get to know everything there is to know about the place where you will spend six or seven hours every weekday, listening, laughing, lounging, liking, loving, and, yes... learning all about life. You will learn about chemistry, math, history, crafts, and, yes, historical drafts. Make the time to learn about your school.

What can happen if you don't do this?

Most high schools offer a wide range of classes and learning activities. Most activities can be found in brochures, catalogs, and other advertising media. However, some programs are very small; very new; or reserved for those students who really want the inside scoop. If you don't actively seek these special programs, you won't find them.

Think about this:

Your high school is not just brick and mortar. Your high school is a community organization with men and women who have all gone to high school... and they care about you.

Show them that you care, too.

Teachers and Nurses...

Two of the world's greatest professions!

GETTING OUT

Appendix 2: THE SOPHOMORE PLAN

NOTES

STEP 1:
Review the Freshman Plan

Perhaps you are reading this book for the first time, or maybe you have had this book for a while, and you are just now getting around to reading it. In either case, review the Freshman Plan.

Think about this:

You are now in high school.

What's next?

Why do this?

Though geared toward the youngest high-school student, the Freshman Plan has fundamental concepts and actions that you will need to accept and understand before going on to the Sophomore Plan. As you continue reading through successive Plans, each Plan will build on concepts discussed in the previous years' Plans. Ideally, you should read this book in the 9th grade. However, until you graduate from high school, all of the information presented in each of the Plans can be applied right now... *today*... regardless of where you are in your college quest.

What can happen if you don't do this?

This book is written specifically to prepare you for the process of applying to college. Specifically, the last five chapters are the exact preparation plan that will take you from high-school freshman to college freshman. If you don't take the time to follow the simple, straightforward plan, you will miss out on very valuable information.

Teachers and students need each other -

...without a student, the teacher doesn't exist;

...without a teacher, the student doesn't exist!

STEP 2:
Begin Researching Scholarships

Though you don't necessarily need them to go to college, scholarships are basically "free money" to help pay for college expenses. There are also loans and grants you may be able to receive.

Why do this?

There are thousands of available scholarships. Some are dependent on specific criteria like grades or athletics. Other "association" scholarships are given to students who are associated with certain organizations. And then there is the "need-based" scholarship, which is based on your financial situation. As a sophomore, you should begin familiarizing yourself with the formats and information required in various scholarship applications. Most require an essay and transcripts; some require letters of recommendation. Don't wait; begin your research *today*.

What can happen if you don't do this?

There are literally thousands and thousands of scholarships available, representing millions, if not billions, of dollars waiting to be given away to students who take the time to research the scholarships, prepare the requested information, and simply submit the application. If you don't do this, you are simply giving away free money!

Think about this...

Scholarships exist at almost every corporation in America. Wal-Mart®, Sears®, McDonalds®, General Motors® and thousands of other companies have a thriving scholarship support program.

Start your research today!

If the best things in life are free,

Get the best education...

With a scholarship!

STEP 3:
Visit a Local College

Back in "Appendix 1: The Freshman Plan," you are advised to simply "Dream." By making the time to visit a college campus, you are bringing your dream one step closer to *your* reality.

Why do this?

Getting to high school was fun, right? Compared to middle school, there is so much to do; new friends to meet; and all kinds of things to learn. Well, college is even better than high school! College will offer even more things to do; many more new friends to meet; and tons of other things to learn. College is so fun that it's almost unimaginable. So take a weekend and pop over to the local college campus. If you can, try to visit more than one college or university campus. And be sure to stop at the financial aid office; start your research today! Dream!

What can happen if you don't do this?

How much do you currently know about college? Many students think college is all about sporting events. And though those exciting events are certainly part of college life, *attending* college is an educational experience designed to create a whole new you. If you miss an early opportunity to visit a campus, you may lose sight of your dream.

Think about this...

In high school, you probably have acquired new friends from across town.

In college, you will acquire new friends from all over the world.

Your college education has the potential to do the same... carry you to a whole new world.

A dream does not necessarily end when you awake.

Live your dream!

STEP 4:
Study the Website of Local College

Believe it or not, many colleges compete for business. They actually want YOU to become part of THEM. And many of today's colleges spend big money on highly informative websites.

Why do this?

If you have a computer at home, great! If you have access to a computer at your high school or at a public library, great! In either case, by logging on to their website, you can actually learn quite a bit of information about your favorite colleges. Yes, there will be links leading to information on upcoming sporting events, campus tours, and general college life. Additionally, you will find telephone numbers, e-mail addresses, and names of people who can offer significant assistance as you navigate through your college application process.

What can happen if you don't do this?

In today's digital age, everything is moving to the Web. And, though you can probably obtain the same information elsewhere, most college websites offer one-stop information access. Many offer prospective students an opportunity to create a student account before actually being enrolled. Don't waste this opportunity!

Think about this...

Like a book, pencil, and paper, the Internet is a tool.

Once you learn how to use all available tools, you will become a skilled architect in the art of learning.

Also be prepared to research available scholarships online.

An Internet is a virtual campus.

Your thoughts of college are also a virtual campus.

Join them all.

STEP 5:
Think "All They Can Do is Say 'No'"

Try this at home: walk over to the bathroom and look in the mirror. Look straight into your eyes and say to yourself, "All they can do is say 'No.'" Know this. Believe this. Live this.

Why do this?

As you begin to get serious about applying to college, ask yourself one simple question: *what will keep me from going to college?* The truth may surprise you. If you actually complete all the actions prescribed in these Plans, you will successfully enter college. So the only thing keeping you from getting into college is YOU. That may seem like a rather bold statement from a guy like me. After all, I don't even know you, right? Here's what I DO know: If *you* never ask, *you* will never receive. All they can do is say "no." Know, believe, and live this!

What can happen if you don't do this?

Is the process really that simple? Can your goals be achieved by following the simple Plans in this book? Yes! But first you must follow the three words at the bottom of the page: **Accept** the fact that these plans *will* work. **Adapt** your life to these Plans. And you will **Achieve** college enrollment. If you don't do this, you deny, maintain, fail.

Think about this...

- MIP #3 -

Ask every question you want to know. Seek scholarships everywhere.

Apply to at least five schools.

All they can do is say "no."

But they will probably say "yes."

Accept

Adapt

Achieve

STEP 6:
Seek a Seat on Student Council

If you really want to make your mark on the world, plan to join the Student Council. You will learn valuable tips on how organizations really work. You will also beef up your college application.

Why do this?

The Student Council plays a very important role at almost every high school (and some middle schools). The Student Council helps facilitate the sharing of student ideas, interests, and concerns with teachers, the principal, and other school administrators. The Student Council also provides a forum for students to raise money for school-related projects. Best of all, your official school record and college application will soon reflect the profile of a person who is interested in the student body, community service, and becoming an adult role model.

What can happen if you don't do this?

Getting elected to the Student Council can be a very competitive challenge. However, the campaign experience alone can teach you quite a bit about organizing events, coordinating efforts, and speaking at public events. Even if you don't get elected, you can still document your unsuccessful campaign experience on your college applications.

Think about this...

By seeking a spot on the Student Council, you are making a bold statement to teachers, guidance counselors, and other administrators.

They will remember you when it comes to writing letters of recommendation.

Lead...

Follow...

Or

Get out of the way.

STEP 7:
Connect With A Graduate Relative

If your parents attended college, great! Ask them to assist you in your college preparation process. However, if they did not go to college, ask them to connect you with a relative who did.

Why do this?

The best advice I can give you is based on the experiences I have had. Likewise, if you have questions about the college application and entrance process, the best person to ask is someone who has "been there, done that." Of course, all of your teachers also have college degrees. Your guidance counselor also has a college degree. And there are numerous people in the community with college degrees. However, as a young student, perhaps you should seek the advice of family members first. Ask them: they will be proud to help!

What can happen if you don't do this?

A trusted family member is more likely to understand you as an individual. Sometimes, teachers and school administrators lose sight of where you are in the whole college-admissions process. If a college-graduate family member is available, but you don't request his or her help, you are wasting a very valuable resource.

Think about this...

All colleges have an Alumni Association. And those associations often give scholarships to relatives of people who have graduated from their college.

Your family's wealth can be measured in knowledge... as well as money.

STEP 8:
Find a Mentor

A mentor is someone who is willing to selflessly guide you to a better life. The trouble with the mentor concept is that most teens erroneously think they already have everything figured out.

Why do this?

If someone had a crystal ball and could see into your future, what would you ask him? If your Fairy Godmother popped up and offered to guide your life by providing direction when you needed it most, would you listen to the old lady? As discussed earlier in this book, sometimes teenagers have a very narrow view of the world. A mentor can help expand your outlook. He or she can objectively suggest ideas, concepts, and alternate paths to seemingly complex solutions. Best of all, a mentor is there for you regardless of whether or not you take their advice.

What can happen if you don't do this?

As noted in the MIP Box above, finding and keeping a good mentor is a very important action on your part. If you decide to take on life without a mentor, you may needlessly fail when you could have succeeded. You will waste valuable time, energy, and effort trying to create or change something that someone has already done *before* you.

Think about this...

- MIP #4 -

The most important point in this entire book is right here:

Find a good mentor...

Listen to him or her...

Follow their advice.

Mentors don't just tell you what to do...

They mend, mold, and mint many.

ACCEPT   ADAPT   ACHIEVE ®

STEP 9:
Consider Various Locations

As you wrap up your sophomore year, begin seriously thinking about where you want to go to school. Some high-school graduates want to stay close to family. Others want to move far away.

Why do this?

When considering your ultimate college, there are so many characteristics to consider. Small college or big university? Coed or single-sex school? College in the north; or summery school in the south? Way out west or just east of your hometown? Technical school or liberal arts academics? These are just a few considerations to review when selecting your college. However, remember that some characteristics may not agree with your overall goals. Moving far away may be fun; but are you really ready for that? I'm sure you are!

What can happen if you don't do this?

As a sophomore, you still have plenty of time before setting your choice of college in stone. However, if you decide to go to a certain school because your best friend is also enrolled at that school, be *absolutely* sure your choice would still be a good choice if you and your friend decided to end the friendship... or your courtship.

Think about this...

There is no "perfect" college.

Focus on getting accepted to at least one or two schools, and then decide which one is better for you and your plans for life.

A trusted friend can fences mend;

A tested friend is a trusted friend.

STEP 10:
Prepare for Graduation NOW!

As a freshman or top grade in middle school, perhaps you did not do as well as you could have. Well, as a student in the tenth grade, now is the time to really get serious about your schooling.

Why do this?

You are in school for only one reason: to learn. Start preparing for your graduation today. Soon, you will graduate from high school... to a real life. And, if you start preparing for graduation today, in three or four years, you can begin preparing for graduation from *college*. You **can** do this! There is no "magic" formula for going to college. You don't need to be super-smart or rich to get into college. You *do* need to be prepared. And, just like the track star who doesn't win races unless she prepares and trains well before the beginning of the race, you should begin preparing for graduation today; now... *this minute!*

What can happen if you don't do this?

If you don't start preparing for college today, when *will* you start preparing for college? In reality, the next two years will soon be consumed by friends, parties, sports, tests, and, in general, high-school life. College may seem far away... but it is far closer than you think. If you don't start preparing today, you may never start. **Never.**

Think about this...

As a 10th grader, your school grades will become part of your permanent record.

Your grades will represent you when you send your application to colleges.

Capital 'T' Truth: You may be cool and pretty, but if your grades are foolish and ugly, colleges will not like you.

Time is a tool.

To be the best creator of you, you should use all available tools.

GETTING OUT

Appendix 3: THE JUNIOR PLAN

NOTES

STEP 1:
Review the Sophomore Plan

Perhaps you are reading this book for the first time, or maybe you have had this book for a while, and you are just now getting around to reading it. In either case, review the previous Plans.

Why do this?

At the beginning of your junior year of high school, you are about 18 months away from graduation. And, though 18 months from now may seem like an eternity, in reality, that's less than two years from now. And once football season turns into basketball and baseball season, you will find yourself one single, solitary year away from high-school graduation. And, believe me; you definitely don't want to start planning the college application process during your senior year of high school. The more you get done this year, the easier things will be next year.

What can happen if you don't do this?

If you don't read the other Plans, you will miss some very valuable tidbits. Some of the information in this Junior Plan assumes you have already completed plans and actions that are suggested in the other two Plans. Connecting with a relative who has graduated from college, for example, is recommended in the Sophomore Plan.

> **Think about this:**
>
> *As a high-school student, you have been receiving information your entire life.*
>
> *As a college student, you will continue to gain valuable knowledge.*
>
> *In life, we never stop learning.*

> *A failure to plan*
>
> *is*
>
> *a plan to fail.*

ACCEPT   ADAPT   ACHIEVE ®

STEP 2:
Review Your Vision

In "Step 2" of the Freshman Plan, I advise you to "Establish and Grow Your Vision." And, after seeing what high school is really like, perhaps you should reevaluate and/or change your vision.

Why do this?

A vision is simply a thought that you or someone else has placed in your mind. Once you write that vision down, it becomes a plan. And, after you have established your vision as a plan, you can begin looking for paths to help you achieve your vision. But remember: your vision is not set in stone. You can change your destination at any time. In fact, though your plan may seem very good, in reality, you are learning many new and different things in high school. Perhaps you will learn a life-changing lesson about physics, psychology, or puppies. Stay flexible.

What can happen if you don't do this?

As you approach graduation, you may begin to feel a sense of urgency or even panic. Relax. Many students think they have to *know* what they want to do with their life before they graduate from high school. In reality, college is a perfect place to figure out life, expand your liberty, and decide how you intend to pursue happiness.

Change is constant.

Expect change.

Deal with changes or changes will deal with you.

ACCEPT   ADAPT   ACHIEVE ®

STEP 3:
Visit a College Financial Aid Office

Okay... now is the time to get serious about financing your college education. In the previous Plans, I talk about familiarizing yourself with the college campus and financial aid office.

Why do this?

By the time you are a high-school junior, you should know the types of financial aid. In the Sophomore Plan, we reviewed the various types of college scholarships. There is also a mixture of government grants and loans. Grants are free money from the federal and state government. Don't fret about getting approved for the loans. As long as you complete the required paperwork and prove you need the money for college, you will likely be approved for a student loan. In many cases, you will be allowed to repay the money AFTER you graduate.

What can happen if you don't do this?

As I stated in the Sophomore Plan, "the only thing keeping you from getting into college is YOU." I make this bold statement because the Financial Aid Office at a local college can show you many options. But if you don't visit the campus or the Financial Aid Office, you may very well end up staying home.

Think about this:

If you start preparing early enough, you may qualify for a totally FREE education.

This may be a rare example, but it does happen!

*Stop by a Financial Aid Office **today** and ask questions!*

Your future starts today.

Where will you be in five years?

STEP 4:
Get SAT/ACT Study Book; Use it!

I personally know people who have owned a copy of the SAT® study book... but have not used it. Unfortunately, when you don't study for the test, you will *not* perform well.

Why do this?

Here's the deal: There is about a 98% chance that your college will require you to take the SAT® or ACT® tests. If someone came up to you and said, "There is a 98% chance that a rock will fall on your home tomorrow..." what would you do? Would you stay in your home tomorrow? You would probably prepare to spend the day somewhere else! Now, I'm not saying "tests are like falling rocks"; but I **am** saying you should study for these tests. Remember: some scholarships are based on your SAT® or ACT® scores.

What can happen if you don't do this?

If you start studying early enough, you will perform well on these almost-mandatory tests. However, if you don't study... or if you wait too late to study for these tests, you will not perform as well as you could have. With so much of your future riding on one specific test, you should start studying now, as soon as you finish reading these words. Your future may very well depend on it.

Think about this:

- MIP #5 -

Grades,
Guidance,
Great Test Scores:

This is what the college acceptance committee will review in your file.

Study.

ACCEPT   ADAPT   ACHIEVE ®

STEP 5:
Take the Right Tests

"Step 4" of this plan advises you to study for the SAT® or ACT® tests. Study. Study. Study. And before you take the official tests, consider taking the Preliminary SAT® (PSAT®) test.

Why do this?

The PSAT® is actually the Preliminary SAT®/National Merit Scholarship Qualifying Test. It is co-sponsored by the College Board and the National Merit Scholarship Corporation. Reasons for taking the PSAT/NMSQT include:

1. Receive feedback on skills required for college study.
2. See which classes you should focus your study efforts.
3. Compare your performance with the performance of other students.
4. Enter a competition for scholarships from the National Merit Scholarship Corporation (for juniors).
5. Help prepare for the SAT by familiarizing yourself with the format of the SAT®.
6. Receive literature from colleges.

What can happen if you don't do this?

If you don't take the PSAT®, you will lose the opportunity to do the items listed above. After reading this book, you are too smart to let that happen.

Think about this:

The SAT® and ACT® are "just" tests. Don't get all nervous or scared when you sign up to take these tests.

The best way to prepare for the SAT® or ACT® is to follow "Step 4" of the Junior Plan.

Also consider taking one or two Advance Placement (AP) Courses (and associated tests).

High-school tests are easier than you think.

For the most part, you are only tested on the topics you have been taught.

STEP 6:
Draft Letters of Recommendation

Relax... there's no requirement to submit letters as a graded assignment. This step is designed to get you familiar with the format for requesting and writing a letter of recommendation.

Why do this?

You should get acquainted with how, why, and when to ask for letters of recommendation. As you prepare to put together your college application, you can also save your letters for scholarship applications to be submitted later. Moreover, some schools require three or more letters from teachers or other community leaders. A well-written letter of recommendation should:

1. Define you as a well-rounded, goal-oriented student with high hopes.
2. Focus on your aptitude, willingness to learn, and seriousness of study.
3. Address your level of maturity and seriousness of purpose.
4. Discuss your leadership ability.
5. Praise your student character.

What can happen if you don't do this?

The biggest part of asking for a letter of recommendation is drafting the initial letter and then discussing the process with the person providing the recommendation. Get started today!

Think about this:

Don't be shy about asking for letters of recommendation.

If you get started early enough, you will have plenty of time to thank your teachers, coaches, and other administrators who may write your letters.

Your letter of recommendation will represent what other people have to "say" about you.

Ask at least five people for letters, and keep the best three letters.

STEP 7:
Reorganize Your Files

"Step 1" of the Freshman Plan instructed you to "Choose a Place to Keep Your Files." As a junior, you are two years older, and you probably have a more focused view of your goals.

Why do this?

If you have not yet selected a place to keep your files, you are probably beginning to see the value of this advice. However, if you have been keeping files in one place since your freshman year of high school, now is the time to go through those files and reflect on your grades, your group activities, and your grand plans for college. Remember: by keeping your information in one, central place, you will not lose anything. You will also quickly find exactly what you are looking for. Over the next 18 months, your files will grow even faster.

What can happen if you don't do this?

Many records and files can be easily reproduced, especially in the digital age that we live. However, if you lose your social security card, driver's license, or other important documents, getting a new one will cost you time and money, as well as the thought of someone else having your personal information.

Think about this:

Getting organized now can prepare you for college.

Once you get to college, time management will become one of your biggest challenges.

However, if you are an organized student, you will have the basis for a successful term.

Get organized!

ACCEPT　　　　ADAPT　　　　ACHIEVE ®

STEP 8:
Beware of Risky Situations

As a teenager, you are very new to the concept of life. As a student in high school, you are a very "senior" member of the school's student organization. But you are still very, very young.

Why do this?

Over the three or four years that you spend in high school, you will probably see, hear, or read about the death of a student at your high school. Death is actually a fact of life. Some people die sooner than others; that's also a fact. As you become a young adult, you will probably be tempted to do all sorts of interesting-but-crazy things. Indeed, there are drugs, alcohol, and other illicit activities. However, sometimes just hangin' out with others can get you into some rather serious trouble. Remember, grades and police records follow you for the rest of your life.

What can happen if you don't do this?

I am not telling you to avoid cool or crazy kids (I, myself, was crazy and cool). I am only asking you to really think about your actions and how those actions can affect the rest of your life. Speeding can be fun; but it can also be deadly. Watching a fight may appear interesting, until a gun appears in the midst. You have only one life to live.

Think about this:

Adults can be very boring killjoys. But try to remember that some adults have seen the best and worst in life.

Some adults are not necessarily smarter than you... they have only travelled the same path as you... long before you have started down that very same road.

"It is the mark of an educated mind to be able to entertain a thought without accepting it."

~ Aristotle

STEP 9:
Volunteer In and Out of School

In "Step 9" of the Freshman Plan, I advise you to plan to get a job. If you already have a job, great! However, you should also volunteer... just pick a worthwhile organization and go!

Why do this?

Maybe you will go to college; maybe you won't. However, someday you *will* have a job. And, in reality, you already have a job: your job is to learn all that you can while you are in school. You are learning how to write well, make sense of math, and, perhaps, how to best use the computer and Internet. But you also need to learn how to follow social rules; how to engage in adult conversation; and how to prepare for your first year in college. Volunteering at a local hospital, church, or school can provide a great opportunity to learn "real-world stuff."

What can happen if you don't do this?

When volunteering for organizations and people, you give a part of yourself. When you give yourself, you gain a sense of compassion for others. And if you don't have any experience as a volunteer, your college application may not compete well with applications from other students who have a documented record of volunteering their time.

Think about this:

When you volunteer, you also add to the network of people who can provide a letter of recommendation for your college and scholarship applications.

To give and expect something in return is natural...

To give and expect nothing in return is supernatural.

ACCEPT   ADAPT   ACHIEVE ®

STEP 10:
Focus DAILY on Your Grades

The next year of school will directly affect your ability to get into college. If your sophomore year was mediocre, make this your best year yet; if it was good, make this your best year *ever*!

Why do this?

By focusing daily on your grades, you will get into the habit of setting great priorities. When you go to college, one of your biggest challenges will be in the area of time management. Indeed, you will have a challenging class or two. You will also have parties to attend; people to meet; places to go; events to attend; and tests to take. Somewhere, in the middle of all that "stuff," you will also have to eat, sleep, study, date, dream, and discuss current events with friends and family. By focusing daily on your grades today, you will prepare well for the future.

What can happen if you don't do this?

Some students think college is different than high school. However, college is also very similar. For instance, you will still be a student; you will still learn from teachers; and you will still receive grades based on your performance on written tests. If you don't have good study habits now, you probably won't have good study habits in college.

Think about this:

You are a student....

You plan to be a college student...

Other than location and material studied, there is no real difference between a college student and a high-school student.

So start training to be a college student today!

The only difference between the "you of today" and the you of five years from now...

is reflected in the changes you start today.

GETTING OUT

Appendix 4: THE SENIOR PLAN

NOTES

SEPTEMBER
Review the Junior Plan

As directed in the previous Plans, make sure you take some time to review, accept, and understand the specific steps of the preceding Plans. Those specific steps are all equally important.

Think about this:

You are now a high-school senior.

Enjoy it!

Why do this?

If you are a high-school senior and are reading this part of *Getting Out* for the first time, please note that the other Plans provide advice on several aspects of the high-school experience. Previous Plans discuss the value of a mentor; the importance of *knowing* your high school; and the significance of time as a tool. As a high-school senior, you are probably looking forward to high-school graduation; that's great! If you have studied and performed well on tests, you have certainly earned the right to graduate. However, be sure to honor your past.

What can happen if you don't do this?

As a senior, some classes may seem challenging; you are to be commended for reaching the highest grade in high school. The next step is "real life." And, though it may seem like you have reached the 12th grade alone, by reading the previous Plans, you will see the importance of others in your life.

Welcome to the school of life...

Are you really ready to graduate?

ACCEPT   ADAPT   ACHIEVE ®

OCTOBER
Finalize

1. Finalize your choice of colleges.
2. Finalize your SAT® or ACT®.
3. Finalize your list of teachers.
4. Finalize your senior plans.
5. Finalize your files.

Why do this?

1. Finalize your choice of colleges:
If you have been researching several different schools, now is the time to cut the list down to less than ten. Remember, many colleges share an application fee. 5 is a good number.

2. Finalize your SAT® or ACT® score:
If previous scores were unacceptable, register now to retake the exams.

3. Finalize your list of teachers:
Whom will you ask? Give them a draft.

4. Finalize your senior plans:
Leadership roles? Employment? Time?

5. Finalize your files:
Keep a separate file for each school.

What can happen if you don't do this?

October is the month to prepare for the actual application to your prospective colleges. November and December will be hectic, especially given the holidays and family events. Try to spend a few days studying for the retake of the SAT®/ACT®. By investing a few days of preparation in October, you will be ready for the takings in November.

Think about this:

Your teachers have gotten to know you quite well. And they really do want you to continue learning and achieving.

Honor them with a request for a letter of recommendation.

Success is the culmination of efforts.

Success is the combination of trial and error.

Success is there; look for it!

ACCEPT   ADAPT   ACHIEVE ®

NOVEMBER
Complete

1. Complete application essays.
2. Complete college applications.
3. Send college applications:
   a. In the mail
   b. Online

Why do this?

This is the critical time for you and your next life as a student. All of the events discussed in the previous plans are put into full effect in the month of November. If you have followed each or at least some of the steps in the previous Plans, you are prepared to finish up your college-application essays, place those applications in the mail, and simply wait for the letters of acceptance. I highly recommend applying to at least 4 schools. The more schools you apply to, the more likely you will receive a letter of acceptance. This is a great month!

What can happen if you don't do this?

Although November is the ideal time to submit applications, you can also participate in a process called "early decision" (ED). When participating in ED, the student agrees to attend that particular school, if admitted. If you decide to do this, be very careful. You *will* be expected to attend that school.

Think about this:

This is your last November as a student in high school. By next Thanksgiving, you will be a college student!

Enjoy your time as a high-school senior. But remember to stay focused on grades.

*You are
a work of art...*

*You have been
created by parents,
relatives, teachers,
and friends.*

Make them proud!

146: GETTING OUT

DECEMBER
Finish

1. Finish a review of achievements
2. Finish a review of alternatives
3. Finish remaining applications
4. Finish administrative thanks
5. Finish semester strong

Think about this:

Many students are clueless when it comes to having good social graces towards their teachers.

Be sure to thank all of your teachers... especially the ones you may not like.

Why do this?

1. *Finish review of your achievements:* Take a break and look at all you have achieved. Be proud of your efforts, as well as your earned accomplishments.
2. *Finish a review of alternatives:* Consider employment opportunities, especially if your grades are not good.
3. *Finish remaining applications:* Submit last-minute school applications.
4. *Finish administrative thanks:* Important: take time to sincerely thank the teachers and administrators who have helped you in this process.
5. *Finish semester strong:* Stay focused on getting good grades!

What can happen if you don't do this?

The holiday break will offer relief in the college-application process. However, quite ironically, the holiday seasons also brings an increased level of stress. Visits from extended family members, high-school mid-term and final exams, and general graduation anxiety can cause stress. If you follow the Plans in *Getting Out*, you can relax a little.

By giving you knowledge...

Teachers invest in your future... as well as their own future.

ACCEPT   ADAPT   ACHIEVE ®

JANUARY
Stay Focused!

Have a little fun. However, you should stay engaged in all of your classes and avoid "senioritis." In reality, some colleges will withdraw their acceptance if your grades drop significantly.

Why do this?

This is the critical time for you and your next life as a student. All of the events discussed in the previous plans are in full effect by the month of January. If you have followed each or at least some of the steps in the previous Plans, you are essentially finished with the college-application process. Don't "throw it all away" by neglecting your studies. As noted above, some schools may actually withdraw letters of acceptance; others may get tough and decrease the amount of financial aid that is initially offered (when you had decent grades). The bottom line: while in school, you are still learning.

What can happen if you don't do this?

Like a job resume, your grade point average (GPA) makes a statement about your efforts in high school. If you lose the focus on your grades, you will risk ruining your GPA. Your high-school GPA is a permanent part of your life; it will follow you to graduate school and beyond (if you decide to enroll).

Think about this:

You have been in school and worked toward graduation your entire life.

As you prepare for the next step, honor your past 11 years of school by focusing on your grades.

Today matters.

FEBRUARY
Obtain Money for College

Start the Free Application for Student Financial Aid (FASFA). If you can start the application earlier, great! However, you will need your family's tax information, available February 1st.

To get federal financial aid, you must:

1. Be a U.S. citizen/eligible noncitizen;
2. Have a valid Social Security Number (unless you're from the Marshall Islands, Micronesia, or Palau).
3. Be registered with Selective Service if you are a male 18-25 years old;
4. Have a high-school diploma; GED Certificate; or have passed an exam approved by the Dept. of Education.
5. Be enrolled or accepted for enrollment as a regular student working toward a degree or certificate in an eligible program at a school that participates in the federal student aid programs.
6. Not have a drug conviction for an offense that occurred *while you were receiving federal student aid* (such as grants, loans, work-study).
7. Not owe a refund on federal grants or be in default on student loans.
8. Demonstrate financial need (except for Stafford Loans) in which federal aid was being received.

Adapted from: www.fafsa.ed.gov

Think about this:

See more info and important links at the **Getting Out** *website:*

www.gettingout.me

Money is not the root of all evil;

The LOVE of money is the root of all evil.

ACCEPT   ADAPT   ACHIEVE ®

MARCH
Quiz a Current College Student

As a high-school senior, you probably have an older friend or two who graduated within the last two years and has gone on to college. Don't be shy; call him or her up and ask questions!

Why do this?

As I stated in a previous Plan, the best advice I can give you is based on the experiences I have had. Likewise, if you have questions about life at college, the best person to ask is someone who has "been there, done that." And, though all of your teachers also have college degrees, there are young, cool people currently attending college in the community where you live. Indeed, as a student, you should seek advice from family members first. However, friends currently enrolled are more likely to provide details on items which you are specifically interested.

What can happen if you don't do this?

Perhaps you have seen movies about life on a college campus. Though fun to watch, those movies are rarely accurate on the details of the fun and feel of what it's like to actually go to college. If you just watch and believe what's on TV, you will set up a false expectation of what it's really like.

Think about this:

Going to college is literally and figuratively like moving to another world.

Perhaps you will live in the dorm on campus; maybe you will live out in town.

Be sure to ask around about your proposed home.

Home is where the heart is.

Remember to visit your old high school and share your new knowledge.

ACCEPT   ADAPT   ACHIEVE ®

APRIL
The Next Level

Acceptance letters will soon start arriving. As soon as you receive the first acceptance letter, announce it to the world. Be proud! Then get started researching the school's financial aid.

Why do this?

An acceptance letter in your hand means you have just been handed the *rights* to go to college. The next step is to choose among the colleges you are accepted, and then obtain the *money* to pay for the education. For most purchases in life, we check to see if we can afford it first. Usually, access to money determines *if* we can have something. However, to pay for college, there is always the option to obtain education loans. Of course, scholarships and grants are preferred methods of payment. But don't be afraid to get a federal educational loan.

What can happen if you don't do this?

As soon as you receive your acceptance letter, thousands of other students are also receiving their acceptance letters. Now there is a race to the finish line. What's at the finish line? Money! It is very important to get your scholarship applications in EARLY and on time. Do not wait! Start your research the day you receive your acceptance letter!

Think about this:

- MIP #6 -

Scholarships and grants are free money;

The longer you wait to apply for your source of financial aid, the less money you will receive.

It's just that simple.

Life is painfully simple.

If you don't do the small, simple things, life will be quite painful!

MAY
Keep in Contact with Your Mentor

As you move toward becoming an adult, you will develop your own sense of the "real world." With greater freedom and fewer teachers around, you will truly be the boss of yourself.

Why do this?

As the "boss" of yourself and your newfound freedom, be very careful and choose a good path in your new life. Every year, thousands of high-school students die because of drug and/or alcohol abuse. Many others will permanently ruin their records due to drinking and driving, fighting, or driving without a license. If you have a mentor, you are far less likely to get involved with these types of behaviors. Keep in mind: A mentor is someone who is willing to selflessly guide you to a better life. More importantly, you really **don't** know everything!

What can happen if you don't do this?

Some teens erroneously think they already have everything figured out. However, keeping your mentor involved in your life is a very important action on your part. If you decide to take on life without a mentor, you will needlessly fail when you could have succeeded. The choice is truly yours.

Think about this:

- MIP #7 -

The second most important point in this entire book is right here:

Find a good mentor...

Listen to him or her...

Follow their advice.

If I only knew then what I do know now,
I would now know what to do about now.

JUNE
Prepare for Graduation NOW!

~ Enjoy your summer ~

Why do this?

~ You deserve it ~

What can happen if you don't do this?

~ You *will* do this ~

Think about this:

You are going to college!

What do you want to be?

With your diploma, you can be anything...

A-N-Y-T-H-I-N-G!

ACCEPT   ADAPT   ACHIEVE ®

THE
END

and

~ A NEW BEGINNING FOR YOU ~

For additional resources

visit

www.GettingOut.me

Acknowledgements

Throughout my existence, I have gained a wealth of knowledge from so many people. Naming each of them within the covers of Getting Out *is impossible. However, given the context of the book, I would be remiss if I did not thank many of those absolutely wonderful teachers within the Buena Vista School District. Specifically:*

Ms. Weathersby; a leader among leaders.

Mrs. Vitany, my kindergarten teacher... she had a truly angelic way of teaching. Mrs. Jackson, from first and second grade, allowed me to read books beyond my academic years, and, as such, fed my voracious appetite for information, knowledge, and understanding.

Mr. Erndt, my third-grade teacher, was essential in helping me gain an understanding of so many fundamentally advanced concepts and applications. Moreover, unbeknownst to me at the time, during my rather rebellious years, Mr. Erndt implored the District on my behalf, beseeching them to reconsider my year-long suspension.

Mrs. Chmielewski, my fifth-grade teacher, was best at helping me learn the value of temperance and "times tables." Likewise, Mrs. Goffney, my sixth-grade teacher, was a pinnacle of patience, persistence, and persuasion. They both have my highest regard.

And, of this I am sure... ask any student who matriculated through the District late in the 20th century, and they will validate this claim:

I owe my appreciation for the English language to Ms. Z. Thompson.

* * *

Special thanks to my dear wife, Delia, who not only provided editorial support for Getting Out*; but she also provided the initial concept for the content and purpose herein. She was actually interested in the stories of my youth; and she has always listened to my sometimes outrageous-but-true stories. Moreover, she inspired me to share my story... in the hopes that others could one day look, live, and love beyond the seemingly hopeless horizon, no matter how near or far.*

~ Thank you, Delia ~

About the Author

John H. Clark III, a career Naval Officer, with a Bachelor of Business Degree from the University of Memphis and an MBA from the Naval Postgraduate School, left high school and travelled the world, soon discovering a true passion for education, empowerment, and altruistic mentoring. An avid speaker, author, and poet, John lives with his wife, Delia, and their two daughters in the Hawaiian Islands.

John H. Clark III
"Back in the Day"

www.ingramcontent.com/pod-product-compliance
Lightning Source LLC
Chambersburg PA
CBHW032102080426
42733CB00006B/382